THINK GOD, TH

THINK GOD,
THINK SCIENCE

Conversations on Life, the Universe, and Faith

Michael Pfundner in discussion with Ernest Lucas

Paternoster:
thinking faith

MILTON KEYNES ● COLORADO SPRINGS ● HYDERABAD

14 13 12 11 10 09 08   7 6 5 4 3 2 1

First published 2008 by Paternoster
Paternoster is an imprint of Authentic Media
9 Holdom Avenue, Bletchley, Milton Keynes, Bucks, MK1 1QR, UK
1820 Jet Stream Drive, Colorado Springs, CO 80921, USA
OM Authentic Media, Medchal Road, Jeedimetla Village, Secunderabad 500
055, A.P., India
www.authenticmedia.co.uk

Authentic Media is a division of IBS-STL U.K., limited by guarantee, with its
Registered Office at Kingstown Broadway, Carlisle, Cumbria CA3 0HA.
Registered in England & Wales No. 1216232. Registered charity 270162

British Library Cataloguing in Publication Data
A catalogue record for this book is available from the British Library

ISBN-13: 978-1-84227-609-9

Design by James Kessel for Scratch the Sky Ltd. (www.scratchthesky.com)
Print Management by Adare
Printed and bound in Great Britain by J.H. Haynes & Co., Sparkford

Contents

Foreword

Have you ever overheard a conversation between other people? Some of these conversations are simply boring but others can be profound. I once sat on a train listening to a 10 minute conversation concerning the quality of the pie that one person was eating! Yet I also remember overhearing two advertising executives discuss how to launch a new soft drink. I remember Michael Parkinson in conversation with Muhammad Ali on his television chat show. And I remember listening to two great theologians discussing models of how God works in the world over a lunch of pizza and chips! There are other conversations which are written down. The philosopher David Hume's *Dialogues Concerning Natural Religion* and indeed the book of *Job* in the Old Testament use conversations to teach very different things about God.

Conversations tell you a great deal, not least in the area of science, religion and the big questions in life. They embody a relationship between science and Christian faith which is not the fierce argument presented in simplistic media stereotypes, but a genuine dialogue where science and Christian faith pose interesting and fruitful questions of each other. In fact, this fruitful dialogue has been going on ever since the rise of the scientific revolution, and is alive today between some of the world's leading scientific minds. It is a dialogue which is genuinely open to learning new things.

In addition, a conversation tells you about the people taking part. You may pick up new ideas from an overheard conversation but you will also learn something more about the participants in it. This is important in the dialogue of science with Christian faith. For Christian faith is not a series of logical propositions to understand the world, it is about the relationship of a man or woman with the Creator God. It is about a combination of evidence and trust, reason and experience. While I am clear that the Christian worldview makes the best sense of the data of this world, one encounters Christian faith in its fullness as it is lived in human beings.

Michael Pfundner and Ernest Lucas allow us to overhear their conversation. It explores the big questions, showing a fruitful dialogue between science and Christian faith. It is a wide-ranging conversation which will inform but also whet the appetite for learning more. It is a conversation that we can have confidence in. Ernest Lucas brings his expertise and experience both as a well known scientist and a well known theologian. Michael Pfundner demonstrates that he knows what the real questions are to ask. But we also see into the lives and faith of these men, in a way that is both challenging and encouraging. They demonstrate a faith which is open to question, seeking truth and finding confidence in Jesus. It is a discussion which is profound and intriguing. The ideal conversation to take with you on a train when the people across the aisle are talking about the quality of pies!

David Wilkinson
David Wilkinson is Principal of St John's College, Durham
University and has doctorates in both theoretical
astrophysics and systematic theology

The Issue

A few years ago, astronomers were busy tracking the path of Asteroid 2003QQ4. A collision with Earth would have equalled the simultaneous explosion of 20 million Hiroshima bombs. The chances of the twain ever meeting, however, were calculated to be 1:909,000. Consequently, 2003QQ4 escaped the attention of the vast majority of earthlings, and in the end even the most dedicated and apprehensive scientist would have lost interest, as the cosmic chunk of rock silently drifted by and disappeared into the depths of space.

Not long afterwards, a Christian magazine published a series of articles on British churches failing to reach the nation. The main problem was seen to be the lack of commitment and convincing lifestyle of its adherents. Though the authors were making some valid points, I could not help feeling that they might be missing the crucial one: the unbroken grip of rationalism on the Western mind and soul. Unquestionably, Christians who walk the talk will, in a sense, be more convincing. Actions may at times speak louder than words, but while a messenger whose deeds match up with their claims will be credited with integrity, there is no guarantee that the message itself will be heeded. I can admire the discipline of a meat-lover turned vegetarian and still carry on ordering lamb shoulder at the pub down the road. First and foremost we assess ideas, not their manifestations; and the idea that the gospel message of Jesus Christ is both culturally relevant and universally true has been contested for long enough to have entered the collective, Western unconscious as something to be treated with suspicion. Therefore, while compromising Christians are naturally regarded as sanctimonious phoneys, devoted

ones may well be considered to be sincere but misled nonetheless. For, after all, what are the odds of a little, blue and white ball
being God's favourite thing in the universe? What are the
chances of that God becoming a man, born of a virgin for that
matter, so he could suffer a cruel death of mystic significance, rise
from the grave and announce he will revisit the planet one day to
judge every human that ever walked on it? These central
Christian tenets, while still affirmed every Sunday by the faithful,
may appear to the sceptical majority as plausible as a close
encounter of the fatal kind with Asteroid 2003QQ4. It looks as if
more ink will be spilt over the struggle of the church to reach the
nation.

For centuries, God was centre stage. Now we prefer him to
hide behind the scenes. When our forebears pondered on their
origin, nature and destiny, their point of reference was religion. It
enlightened them on the mysteries of the universe and showed
them how to live and how to die. The church mediated between
heaven and earth. The clergy drove culture and governed society
along with their worldly counterparts. Evidently, the church of
today has lost most of its former spiritual and social authority;
but the actual question is: has God himself as we knew him had
his day? Yes, spirituality is still around, but much of it seems
fuzzy, trend-driven and privatised. As for the Christian faith,
however, which once had a universal impact, is it only a matter
of time until it silently fades into oblivion?

The loss of the God of our forebears comes at a price. The existential malaise that haunts our secular new world warrants the
question: did we leave God behind all too lightly? But then, even
if losing their faith might make some people miserable, what
would it prove? Even if we could show that, overall, religion did
in fact contribute to the well-being of individuals and societies,
the underlying question would not go away: is there any rational basis for the faith that shaped Western civilisation for
nearly two millennia? Many would argue that the latter part of
that period, driven by science and reason, has slowly but surely
built a pretty convincing case against the God of the Bible; some
would add, against God, full stop. But then, how did we get
here? Are today's widespread religious relativism, agnosticism
and even atheism nothing but the inevitable result of humanity

coming of age? Are current feelings of disorientation and gloom mere growth pains, as we slowly progress from abandoned, infantile concepts of a cosmic father-figure towards a level of human independence that courageously asserts itself even in the face of ultimate futility?

How, then, if at all, are we to 'think God' in the twenty-first century? Is the Christian message of a benevolent creator, an intentional universe and a life that has meaning still defensible? The question is at the heart of this book. We shall look at it from a scientific and a theological perspective. By the way, this is a starter for the layperson, rather than a three-course meal for the specialist; an introductory conversation outlining the issues, not a full treatise of each one of them.

If you still find yourself grappling with questions, the book is likely to engage you, whether you are a Christian who struggles to reconcile heart and intellect, or simply someone who is tired out by the dance of happy consumerism on the Western dog-eat-dog stage and led to wonder whether spirituality could be among the few things that make life worth living. On the other hand, anyone who seeks to respond to the God question in purely rationalist terms will almost certainly put the book down disappointed. This holds not only for the convinced sceptic but also the believer whose apologetic boils down to the elimination of uncertainty through an allegedly watertight system of facts. To the one, trust is the deadly sin, to the other it is doubt. As I understand Christian faith, however, it is neither a leap into the dark in the face of counterevidence, nor the inevitable verdict in the face of positive proof. To the secular fundamentalist, my position is a cop-out, for it allows for an unobservable, supernatural dimension. To the Christian fundamentalist, it smacks of questioning God's revelation, because science operates on the basis of looking at nature's riddles without invoking the existence or action of God, and of compromising with worldviews that have long ceased to be handmaids of theology. Walking between the frontlines of secular and religious fundamentalism carries the risk of being attacked from both sides; but in times when the dialogue between science and faith is becoming more strained, any contribution towards mutual understanding, even on a scale as modest as the one you hold in your hands, is worthwhile.

My following conversation with biblical scholar-cum-bio-chemist, Reverend Dr Ernest Lucas, without whom this book could not have been written, reflects questions that have preoccupied me ever since I became a Christian. I believe that though nowadays many would somewhat disdainfully call them 'modernist', they are in fact timeless and therefore as valid as ever. For if the Christian faith goes beyond private conviction and personal experience we must examine questions pertaining to rationality, objectiveness and truth. Moreover, I am wary of any church teaching or practice that equates spiritual maturity with dodging the probing questions of the mind, whether they are raised by scientists, philosophers, a sceptical friend or simply our own common sense. If the gospel of Christ is worth anything, surely it will stand up to our attempts to make sense of it.

Thinking God's Thoughts

Dr Lucas, the argument between faith and science has been fought on the Western, post-Enlightenment stage more than in many other parts of the world. So, to some, it may come as a surprise that modern science arose and began to flourish in Western Europe in a way that it did not in other parts of the world – not in spite of, but because of, Christianity.

Well, we need to start out by asking 'What is modern science?' One of the markers of modern science is the 'mathematisation' of our way of looking at the world. Of course mathematics was important in Ancient Greece and other cultures, but more as a philosophy and as a tool rather than applied to what, by the Middle Ages, was called 'natural philosophy' – which was a specific way of looking at the natural world. In late medieval Europe people began to use the process of quantifying as they studied nature; they sought to use mathematics as a kind of language in which to put their understanding of the world. For instance, by the late Middle Ages, people stopped studying animals to learn moral lessons from them. In medieval encyclopaedias of nature, an essential part of the article on each animal had been a moral lesson to be drawn from this animal.

Like Aesop's fables.

Yes, an upgraded form of Aesop's fables, which diverted people
away from what we would consider to be a scientific way of looking at the world. That changes by late medieval times – as
Harrison[1] argues – partly as a result of the Protestant move from
allegorising the Bible to what Luther and Calvin described as
reading the Bible in its natural sense, in terms of the grammar
and history and so on. That different approach to interpreting the
Bible, Harrison says, has a spillover into interpreting reality. The
natural world is no longer studied because of the moral and spiritual lessons that can be derived from it, but as something to be
studied in its own right at a physical, material level.

*In the early stages of the universities, mathematics was very much con-
sidered as a tool . . .*

And the mathematician was fairly low down the pecking order,
which changed with Galileo[2] and Kepler,[3] and really as early as
Copernicus.[4] His mathematical model, with the sun at the centre, was
simpler and made it easier to calculate the movement of the planets.
Therefore, he concluded that it was a closer match to reality. He
regarded mathematics not just as a useful tool but as a description of
reality; and this carried on with Kepler and Galileo. Galileo's initial
appointment was that of a mathematician, but he got into trouble
because he kept critiquing Aristotle. You weren't supposed to do
that.[5] And when he got his job with the Medici family, he insisted that
his title was 'philosopher', not 'court mathematician'. In the context
of the time that was quite a major shift. Kepler, too, when he was
employed by the Holy Roman Emperor in Prague, insisted on being
the emperor's philosopher and not his mathematician.

*In other words, the late Middle Ages witnessed the development of
'mathematisation' – filtering one's view of the world through the lens of
rational mathematics. Mathematics was no longer just a practical tool
but had begun to attain a higher status.*

Correct. And there's one more thing we need to consider: the
shift away from deductive reasoning, which for many Ancient

Greek philosophers had been the primary way of finding truth. They assumed the existence of eternal forms and thought that these were reflected by the physical world. So they started out by intuiting the eternal forms and then deducing conclusions from them. That changed at the dawn of modernity. Francis Bacon[6] argued that we should observe and collect evidence by looking at small areas of reality; and only then should we induce an overall pattern on the basis of what we find. Next we go on to make further observations, to see whether our conclusions were valid or not. In other words, people started observing the world, asking, 'What is reality really like?'

I think what we have in many cultures before is technology, rather than science. People were concerned with, say, metallurgy or astronomy for practical reasons; they wanted to be able to make better weapons and ploughshares and predict the seasons. Of course they had religious motives as well; for instance, one of the main concerns of medieval astronomy was to fix the date of Easter. But gradually science developed not just for instrumental reasons, but as a way of describing reality.

What about the social and economic factors? How did they influence the rise of modern science?

The voyages of discovery are one aspect to consider. They were done primarily for economic reasons, but they also opened people's eyes to a world that they hadn't known about. Remember the medieval encyclopaedias; well, suddenly people were introduced to all sorts of strange creatures, and that got them to look at this new world simply because it was interesting, and not to draw moral or spiritual lessons from it.

Essentially, there needs to be a culture with enough wealth for there to be a sufficient number of people who are free to pursue science. There need to be patrons with the money and the interest to employ people like Galileo and Kepler. There needs to be a society with enough excess wealth to found universities that do more than simply train people for the church, which happened initially, but where large numbers of the wealthier classes can go to be educated.

*And then there is the different approach to science that you mentioned
a moment ago – science in Ancient Greece remaining essentially at the
level of technology.*

This is to do with the world-view of a culture. The Babylonians had
achieved a considerable development in mathematics, which
allowed them to solve quite complicated quadratic equations,
which in turn arose from the need to measure fields and so on. But
then they looked at the heavens for religious reasons, because they
believed that the moving planets were deities and, by observing the
movements, they could work out what was on the deities' minds.
Their observational astronomy was quite sophisticated, but it never
developed into proper astronomy; instead, by 400 BC we end up
with a sophisticated level of astrology, which the Greeks then took
over.

In those cultures the gods are kind of superhuman beings and,
like human beings, they are unpredictable. We can understand
other people to some degree but they always surprise us. Since
the Babylonians and Greeks expected the gods to surprise them,
they didn't look for what we would call natural laws. They just
observed, and anything that would have been out of the ordinary,
such as an eclipse, was the gods doing something unusual,
because they had something special to say.

In early Islamic culture we get the opposite extreme. Islam had
taken over some of the major centres of learning, such as
Baghdad or Alexandria, which gave them access to Greek material in the libraries. They translated it into Arabic and made good
use of it. This resulted in quite rapid developments in chemistry,
astronomy, mathematics and so on and, at that stage, Arabic culture was way ahead of European culture in its development of
science. But then it began to slow and ground to a halt. Why?
Historians of science and historians of Islam both point to a
change in the dominant Islamic theology; I've read Islamic scholars themselves who say this. A group of Islamic philosophers,
such as Al-Ghazzali (1058–1111), took the lead, emphasising two
things. Firstly, that divine sovereignty is so prevalent that every
event is directly caused by Allah. If we believe that, we won't go
looking for what we call natural causes. Secondly, they stress the
inscrutability of Allah. Humans can't understand the mind of

Allah and it becomes almost blasphemous to seek to understand why things happen. In other words, we get this break on scientific endeavour because it comes to be seen as something un-Islamic. Articles in the *New Scientist* over the past few years have asked the question why, in the modern context, science isn't a successful, major endeavour in Islamic universities. The answer seems to be found in the attitude that, in one sense, science is un-Islamic.

Whereas in medieval Christianity the paradigm shift seems to have been the opposite: away from the mystery of the world towards its rationality.

Which leads us to the question that from the 1920s and thirties historians of science began to ask: 'Why did the new scientific approach occur in a Christian, Westernised culture in a way it hadn't in other cultures, such as Ancient Greece or Babylon?' The early, modern scientists identify three elements, all of which go back to the Bible.

Firstly, the world was made by a rational God. For example, when we read in the Old Testament books of Proverbs and Psalms about the wisdom of God as he created the Earth, they speak of a world that is rational because of its rational creator. Unlike the Babylonian myths of the gods, the Bible also stresses the faithfulness of the creator.

Secondly, according to the Bible we humans are made in the image and likeness of God. Thirdly, therefore, we can expect to understand the world that God has created. In Babylonian religion, we don't have that idea at all. The ruler is the image of the gods, but only in the sense of being their representative. This is not the same as what, say, Thomas Aquinas[7] meant when he linked the divine image with human rationality that distinguishes us from animals. In Judaism and Christianity, God is both sovereign and rational. We can't dictate what God would do; whereas in, say, Platonic philosophy, there is the idea of eternal forms which the creator god, who is subject to the 'top god', has to follow. We as humans can sense the eternal forms, so we can say what the creator god should have done. In the Judeo-Christian tradition, however, God is rational. We are made in the image of God and can therefore understand what God has done, but only after the event; God is free to do what he likes. Therefore we have to go and look at what God has done; hence the stress on observation and experiment that came later. If we read the early modern scientists, they are aware of the difference of this Bible-based approach from the Aristotelian science that was pursued in the universities of the day, and they say that the trouble with the Aristotelian philosophers is that they don't go and look. We can't assume what God would have done; we've got to go and look what God has done. We will be able to understand it when we see it – at least in measure – but we have got to go and look.

One of the striking examples of this is Johannes Kepler, a very devout Christian, who is one of my favourite early modern scientists. He spent five years trying to find a geometrical shape that would fit the data with regard to the orbit of Mars. He got the data from Tycho Brahe, one of the greatest observational astronomers, and this data didn't fit a circle. Kepler was sufficiently confident in Brahe's measurements that he thought this was significant. It took him five years – of course he didn't have modern calculators but only pen and paper – to work out that the right shape was an ellipse. When he wrote this up in his book, Harmonice Mundi (1619), he said quite openly that what kept him going for five years was that geometry was something in the mind of God which could be understood by the human mind, because we are made in the image and likeness of God. This is one of the prime motivations of the early modern scientists: they are sure that they will be able to understand the world.

So, unlike today, science and faith mutually enhanced each other.

Very much so! Moreover, those scientists were motivated by the idea that something could be done to ameliorate the fallen state of the world. The saving work of Christ was seen to have repaired the spiritual damage, but people felt they had a responsibility to repair the physical damage. Bacon stated this as one of the reasons why we should pursue science: to work with God to repair the damage done to creation. There we have another strong, religious motivation for doing science. Later, of course, this became secularised as the drive to make life easier and to provide us with a more comfortable existence.

But it has to be said that by the time Galileo backed Copernicus' claim that the Earth was not at the centre of the universe, the church had begun to turn against science.

The Roman Catholic Church at the time was in a somewhat apprehensive position. Therefore, threats to its authority were a sensitive matter. But initially Galileo was a threat to the university system. As a student he got the nickname 'arguer' or 'wrangler' because he was constantly questioning Aristotle's physics. As a mathematician he pushed this critique further. But as mathematicians were low down in the ranking order and merely supposed to provide mathematical models, they weren't meant to comment on reality. Galileo nevertheless insisted on talking about reality and saying that Aristotle had got it wrong. Once he had become court philosopher, he had more freedom to do this and all the way through we see that it's the academic establishment that countered him.

Another thing they didn't like about him is that he wrote in Italian, not in Latin, which meant that the ordinary people could read it. The classic case was that he published a book which disproved Aristotle's hydrostatics in Italian, with experiments that people could do in their homes to show that Aristotle was wrong. That made him very unpopular with the university professors, and an anti-Galileo league began to form that unsuccessfully sought to refute him. So it seems to have been the university establishment that brought in the church to attack him and instigated a Dominican priest to preach a sermon against him.

It was the university faculty that complained to the Duchess Cristina that Galileo's claims were contrary to Scripture. So his first major apologetic work is a letter to the duchess, explaining how, as he saw it, what he was doing was not opposed to Scripture.

Was he being diplomatic or was his faith beginning to crumble?

As far as I can understand it, he never wavered in his Christian faith. He saw himself as having a role in preventing the church from making a fool of itself. He was certainly not the most diplomatic of persons. In his writings he could be extremely arrogant – another reason why he got into trouble with the church. Initially he appears to have had quite good relationships with the Jesuits who, at first, seemed quite impressed with what he had found. But he got into some argument with them over his observation of sunspots, and it really seems to have been his arrogance that turned them off and made friends into enemies. As a result, they may well have instigated the banning of his book *Dialogue Concerning the Two Chief World Systems*, which eventually led to his trial.

So there is a whole complex of factors and of course the intellectual snobbery, because he was not a biblical scholar; what right had he to write a tract about the interpretation of Scripture? Doing so got him into trouble with the magisterium of the church, as interpreting the Bible was their job, not that of a mere mathematician. In his letter to the duchess, he quotes from Augustine[8] and various other theologians in his own support.

Is that the context in which he said 'The Bible tells us how to go to heaven, not how the heavens go'?

The quote is often attributed to him, but is actually from a leading churchman – obviously someone who didn't manage to convince his fellows. Anyway, all this didn't do Galileo much good. The final nail in his coffin was that he presumed on his friendship with the Pope, a Florentine who had been a friend at the Medici court. Galileo thought that the tides proved that the Earth moved; the Pope, on the other hand had a pet theory of the tides which was rather different and, in his book *The Dialogue Concerning the Two Chief World Systems*, Galileo makes the Pope's theory look stupid.

The Inquisition recommended a punishment that was much more lenient than the one which was eventually handed down by the Pope. And some people say that Galileo's attack on Aristotelian philosophy implied an indirect attack on core Catholic teaching. If Aristotle was wrong, this would undercut the doctrine of transubstantiation, which depended on Aristotle's distinction between essence and appearance. In the Catholic Eucharist, once bread and wine have been blessed and the Holy

Spirit is invoked to come down on the bread and wine, they are changed into the body and blood of Christ. They don't look any different, but they've changed in essence. That made sense if one accepted Aristotelian philosophy, which makes a sharp distinction of the essence and the appearance of a thing. But if Aristotle was wrong in his physics, how did one trust the rest of his philosophy? This was a big debate after the Reformation, between Catholics and Protestants, about what happens when you bless the communion elements, bread and wine; because Protestants agree on there being no change in essence. So there are major implications for this central Christian doctrine in Galileo's attack on Aristotle's physics in the public realm.

What about Copernicus? He didn't agree to the publishing of his revolutionary book that banned the Earth from the centre of the universe until he was lying on his deathbed. Didn't he fear the church authorities as well? Didn't he sense the tension between faith and science?

I don't know how far it was a tension between faith and science or how far it was his own feeling that the academic establishment would not accept his theory. And it's hard to distinguish that establishment from the church, because the universities were originally seats of theology to prepare people for priesthood, so it's a fine line to draw. He might well have been aware that the church, which had accommodated the Bible to Aristotle, would object. They were reading Scripture in the light of Aristotle's Earth-centred cosmology. Verses such as 'The LORD . . . has established the world; it shall never be moved' (Ps. 93:1, NRSV), or the image of the sun going across the heavens like a bridegroom (Ps. 19:5) all fitted in fine with Aristotle. Copernicus would have been aware that the suggestion that it was the Earth that moved and not the sun would be hard to defend in the light of Scripture, and that making this major break with Aristotle would mean taking on the whole academic establishment, and not least the mathematical system of Ptolemy – based on Aristotle – that was used to calculate the date of Easter. Clearly, this was not just about the church, but the whole intellectual tradition of the late Middle Ages.

Nonetheless, in the twentieth-century play, Life of Galileo *by Bertolt Brecht,[9] Galileo concludes that, given what he has seen through his telescope and the conclusions that he has drawn, it is time to abolish the idea of heaven.*

That play draws out something of the intellectual mindset that Galileo was fighting in his day and it's helpful for people to see that. But Brecht also transposes it into a twentieth-century setting, which distorts it to some extent. For example, his presentation of the Roman Catholic Church as an institution seeking to suppress truth is influenced by the spectre of Nazism which threatened Europe in 1939 when Brecht wrote the first draft of the play. I think this leads to an over-simplified and over-polarised picture of the relationship between Galileo and the church.

As for Kepler, he backed Galileo and didn't see a contradiction between faith and what was in fact the dawn of modern science. If he knew all we know about the universe and physics, would he still say the same?

Well, that's impossible to tell, but I would hope so. One of Kepler's best known sayings is 'Lord, I'm thinking your thoughts after you.' He had a priestly sense of seeking to understand the patterns that God had put into the world and to mediate these to humankind. Others would use the idea of the two books of revelation – the Bible and nature. Galileo, in his letter to the Duchess Cristina, talks about the fact that revelation in Scripture and revelation in nature ought to be compatible, and if we find a contradiction, we must revise our understanding and interpretation of Scripture. Kepler would have had the same sort of attitude; we look at Scripture in the light of scientific discovery and do not just hand down fiats from the biblical scholars saying, 'This is how we read Scripture, therefore you must be wrong.'

Doublethink?

You have shown that faith and science co-existed in the late Middle Ages and that indeed the Christian belief in a rational creator and a rational world encouraged people to look at the world through the lens of reason and to use observation and experiment to find out what the world is really like. But gradually there is a rift between the two.

There are a number of factors that led to this rift. Firstly, the question of authority became a major issue; particularly in Catholic Europe, the stress of authority lay on the church, which resulted in an increasing antagonism towards the church in Catholic countries such as France. The church insisted on keeping its hold on the interpretation of the Bible and therefore there was no free debate. Meanwhile, the success of science was giving people growing confidence in human reason. I see this move towards rationalism as a move towards setting up a separate authority of the human mind, over and against the authority of the church. So there's initially a division between academia and the church and not so much science and Christianity, but the two are so wound up that it is difficult to separate them. This seems to be different in Northern Europe, where the Reformation has moved, at least in theory, the authority from the church to the Bible.

But in Britain the clash happened, certainly by the nineteenth century.

To some extent. But that was due to the church's control of education – in other words, not because it was deliberately suppressing science, but because it was largely biased towards arts and humanities. As a result, the burgeoning scientists felt that they were not being appreciated enough in the academic establishment and saw the church dominance in academia as something they needed to fight against in order to raise their own academic status. Anti-clericalism arose in Victorian England with the Church of England's dominance particularly in the universities of Oxford and Cambridge and the school system, which was largely being run by the church until the late nineteenth century. Darwin's supporter Thomas Huxley set himself up as a priest of nature – in a very different way to Kepler. Huxley held Sunday schools to teach science, and what he tried to get across was that science ought to be brought into the curriculum in a new way. And he – I think, wrongly – tars the church with the brush of being anti-science.

Related to the problem of church authority and influence, there is, of course, the issue of the authority of the Bible.

Which we see in the trial of Galileo, who was condemned because what he taught was against philosophy and Scripture as understood at the time. That was compounded because of the church's understanding of its right to interpret Scripture. In Protestant countries, the stress lay on the right of individual people to read and interpret the Bible for themselves. Consequently, there was a greater willingness to accommodate the understanding of Scripture with the growth of science. We see this initially in the area of geology regarding the age of the Earth and the biblical story of Noah and the Flood. By 1800, biblical scholars were more prepared to re-examine their understanding of the biblical texts and to accommodate the idea that the Earth was much older than previously thought.

Good old Archbishop Usher . . .

Yes, in the eighteenth century, the Archbishop of Armagh had calculated that the Earth was created on 10 October 4004 BC or something like that. But by 1800, Christian scholars had begun to get involved in geology. Many of the natural philosophers of the time were clergymen, because they had the time and the training. And this is where the idea cropped up that the six days of creation in the book of Genesis might be not literal days but great ages. So these people were willing to adjust their understanding of Scripture in the light of other evidence.

But what is the tipping point? Where does the dominance of science lead people to relegate faith to the subjective and speculative?

It arose out of the scientific method of quantifying and measuring. When the Royal Society of London for the Improvement of Natural Knowledge was founded in Britain in 1660, the constitution stated that politics and religion should not be discussed, because the society was dealing with that which we can observe, measure and count. What they were saying was 'we are limiting ourselves to an area of exploration, without denying the importance or reality of

things we can't investigate'. So they did their science within a
wider framework of a Christian world-view, but as science became
more and more successful and more and more dominant in people's thinking, that's where we get the shift – I suppose as early as
the 1700s – that theology is seen as being less successful than science and therefore becomes an area of uncertainty and ultimately
an area of unreality because it is closed to the scientific method.

With theology, we're always up against 'my thoughts are not
your thoughts . . . says the LORD' (Is. 55:8, NRSV). Theologians talk
about mystery, but from the point of view of rationalism, which
developed on the basis of science, mystery becomes nonsense.

How did Christians respond to this trend?

In a sense, they shot themselves in the foot. To some degree, one
has to blame Isaac Newton.[10] He realised that gravity caused a
problem for the stability of the solar system. Initially, he carried
out his calculations with the sun as the dominant gravitational
source and he was able to derive the movements of the planets
from Kepler's laws; that's fine. But then he says, 'Hold on a
moment! The planets are also attracting each other; so that's
going to disturb their orbits around the sun. So how come it's a
stable system?' And since Newton couldn't solve the problem
mathematically, he suggested that God must intervene periodically.

The God of the gaps . . .

Yes, he came up with this kind of apologetic that says, there is this
which we cannot understand as scientists, therefore God must
step in. Ninety years later, with better mathematical understanding and tools, Pierre de Laplace[11] would show that there is something called resonance that enables the solar system to settle
down to be a stable system. Laplace pointed this out in his book
and dedicated it to Napoleon, and the story goes that Napoleon
– I very much doubt that he read it, but he was probably given an
executive summary – has an interview with Laplace and asks
where God is in all this; and Laplace replies, 'Sire, I have no need
of that hypothesis.' And in our modern day, I've heard Richard

Dawkins[12] say more than once that Christians were people who sought for God in the cracks of the universe and that, thank God, the cracks kept closing.

Let's go back in time for a moment. What about Christian thinkers such as Abelard,[13] Ockham[14] or Descartes?[15] Wasn't it they that set the trend of relying on reason, logic and scientific observation? After all, Abelard said that it was through questioning and doubting, not faith, that we gain understanding; in other words, suddenly we're not starting with God as a given, but everything can be questioned and analysed by the human mind.

Yes, Abelard did turn the famous saying of Athanasius,[16] 'I believe, so that I may understand' on its head. And, yes, Ockham's famous razor – look for the simplest explanation – is going to have its problems in theology, because we're dealing with the finite human mind trying to understand the infinite. I think, in theology and reason there must always be room for mystery, for recognising that there is a limitation to human understanding, because we are finite creatures and God is infinite. We can have a certain degree of understanding, but we are going to reach an area where we go beyond what we can tie down in logic and that's when, sometimes, we have to make that difficult decision between what is mystery and what is simply nonsense. And there's a fine line to be drawn there.

With Descartes I certainly see a stress on rationality – 'I think, therefore I am' – that elevates human reason to another authority. In his own mind, he may have been able to embrace that concept within a wider Christian philosophy. But he almost sold the pass in his insistence that we must have a rational system of thought – a system which, it seems to me, he sought to build upon a kind of Euclidian model of axioms. In other words, just as Euclid had done with his geometry, Descartes approached the God question by starting with a small number of assumptions, or beliefs, and then tried to deduce a system of ideas from that basis. We can see a parallel, if not a direct line, with later deism in the eighteenth century, which would accept God as a creator somewhere out there, like a mechanic who put together a machine, but we just recognise his existence and that's it.

You mentioned Richard Dawkins. He is convinced that there is enough mystery in the universe and that no religious mystery needs to be manufactured on top of that.[17]

I guess the sort of mystery he is thinking of is the one that scientists often talk about nowadays – that a lot of science is counter-intuitive. There's the famous quote about quantum mechanics that whoever says they understand quantum mechanics clearly doesn't, because it's so counter-intuitive. In theology, of course, mystery has a deeper root because of the belief that there is a transcendent being out there. Theologians have drawn the parallel of the transcendence of one human being over another; the recognition that another human being is beyond our full understanding. Human beings surprise us, however well we think we know them. So theologians say if God is the Supreme Being, it's unsurprising that God surprises us and goes beyond our grasp. Dawkins' mystery is empirical; we find the world surprising at times. And I would add, well maybe, just maybe, this does point to a creator. There are pointers within science that at least ask the God question, and we need to ponder on it if we're willing to move in a thoughtful way from physics to metaphysics.

To summarise, why is it that today faith and science seem so far apart?

Well, we can't get away from the fact that, in most religions, there is the concept of revealed truth because of the belief in a transcendent reality, a God about whom we can't find out for ourselves. In the Judeo-Christian and Islamic traditions this is seen by way of a divine being communicating with human beings in one form or another. The conflict has to some extent arisen by trying to use revealed truth as a basis for scientific truth – going back to Galileo and his opponents quoting from the Psalms to prove that the Earth doesn't move. But then it's interesting to see how Calvin, for example, deals with apparent contradictions between the Bible and his own knowledge about nature. Genesis 1 speaks of two 'great lights' (sun and moon), whereas in Calvin's day people had worked out that Saturn was bigger than the moon. But that didn't worry Calvin, because he concluded that the writers of the Bible had written about the natural world as they saw it, and not in scientific terms. It's the language of appearance and not the language of essence; Calvin was using the Aristotelian terms. So, while that strand of thinking is there in Christianity, there is also a minor strand that tends to read the Bible more literally in relation to the physical world. So we say, this is revealed truth and it is at odds with scientific truth, and therefore we again have to choose between two authorities. That's just what Augustine tried to avoid, by making the point that we should not tie our understanding of Scripture to a particular theory of the natural world, in case that theory changes and we then bring the Bible into disrepute. He's very upfront about that. But many Christians haven't heeded his warning.

How does the concept of natural theology fit into this?

It's a very fuzzy term. My understanding of it would be the idea that, by looking at the world, we can gain some understanding about the nature of the creator. That goes back to the way the Ancient Greeks thought to prove the existence of God. Later on it appears as one of Thomas Aquinas' five proofs for the existence of God. When we look at nature and humans we can learn something about the God who created them. For instance, God would be seen as a moral being, because a sense of morality is inherent in human beings. That seems to me to face two difficulties. One, we are finite beings and God is infinite. Theologians recognise this and are distrustful of natural theology on those grounds; for on the basis of the world and people we know the most we can say is what God is not. Others take a more positive view and say we can extrapolate; that is, we can draw conclusions about God from the world around us. The second problem in the Christian tradition is the belief in the fallen state of human beings. Not only are our minds finite but they are also fallen; as the apostle Paul says in his letter to the Romans, chapter 1, we have a tendency to suppress the truth. That would be Karl Barth's[18] view, quite strongly, that in our fallenness we can't understand God, whereas the Catholic approach taken from Thomas Aquinas takes a more positive view; namely that the human mind is not so affected by the Fall and can therefore comprehend something of God.

What about science itself? Has it taken the place of religion as human-
ity's ultimate key to unlocking the riddles of God's existence and the
world in which we live?

In the British system at least, we do science without doing any
philosophy. Certainly my experience of science through school
and university was that we were never made to stop and think
about the scientific method and its weaknesses and limitations. I
think that has changed to some degree and certainly in Europe,
where students of science will also do a course in philosophy. It
was really Francis Bacon who had started this off by stressing the
objectivity of science as opposed to the humanities and arts. But
David Hume[19] began to critique this quite strongly saying that we
couldn't prove rigorously that the inductive method worked.[20]
He accepted it on empirical but not on logical grounds. In other
words, experience might lead us to draw certain conclusions,
which might be true or not. For instance, Hume pointed out that,
however often the sun rose in the morning we couldn't say with
certainty – the certainty of the deductive philosophers – that it
would rise the next day. We could only say that that was our
expectation. So the basis of science is expectation rather than
truth. We recognise a pattern and we assume that it will continue
and, going back to the early modern scientists, they assumed it
on the basis of a faithful creator. But once we remove the faithful
creator, we're just left with this thing hanging in the air.
Philosophers of science begin to grapple with these issues and to
recognise David Hume's critique. The traditional view of science
has been that it gives us positive truth. We carry out our experiments and make our observations, discover patterns, express
them in a law, possibly a mathematical equation, and from that
obtain deductions which are then tested and, if the test works,
we've proven our law. That's the positivist view of science. But if
we think of it in the light of Hume's critique, all we've done is to
establish that so far this law holds and that, who knows, tomor-
row, or next year, someone will do an experiment which will disprove it.

As with Newton's physics, for instance; it works perfectly well for steam
trains and planets, but less so in the subatomic realm.

Well, in the nineteenth century, leading physicists like Lord Kelvin implied that physics was more or less finished. He said that there were only one or two clouds on the horizon of science, no bigger than a man's hand (he referred to the story of Elijah in the Bible), but that basically physics was wrapped up. A few years later, along comes Einstein and blows the whole thing apart. Newton had reigned supreme for 200 years, but now people realised, not that he was wrong, but that he was insufficient. His laws were not wrong but limited.

Then we get Karl Popper[21] saying that if we can't prove laws, perhaps the test of what is scientific is that we can imagine a way in which a law can be disproved. And as time goes on, we grow in confidence about the things that haven't been disproved, but still we can't be absolutely confident about them.

Another aspect to consider is the rise of the critique of the sociology of science, which questions how our scientific approach is influenced by who we are, by our 'sitedness' in culture.

Finally, since Freud and the beginnings of psychoanalysis, the question has been asked, are the patterns we observe in nature really there? What is the relationship between reality and the picture the mind paints of reality? Again, the early modern scientists would have referred to us having been made in the image of the creator. Remove that and we have got a problem; are the patterns real or are we imagining them?

As a layperson, I observe that the critique of science is rarely popularised; by and large, the public is given the impression that even though science hasn't got all the answers yet, they will be found eventually and that by solving the ultimate riddles of the universe, science may even eventually replace religion.

I think that's weaker now than it was twenty or thirty years ago. Our culture seems to be getting a bit more schizophrenic about science. And yet it does seem to me that, as you say, for a large proportion of the population the one area of authority still seems to be science, which is different from the authorities of religion and ideology – Buddhism, Marxism or New Labour. To some extent we are still hanging on to the Enlightenment idea that this is the only area of truth, and that all other areas, like religion, are about opinions and preferences. You are free to have your opinion, but don't try to force it on me.

What about the popular view that in a scientific age, Christianity is so far behind the times? Dawkins, for example, accuses religions of having a 'poky, little medieval view of the universe'.[22]

I think that's rather unfair. Many Christians have taken on the view of modern science of a great cosmos. If at all, I think the poky medieval view is there as part of a very recent phenomenon, namely post-modernism, which in a sense is very insular and self-centred – the only truth is my truth. The world is shrunk down to my world. Yes, we get this amongst Christians, but not necessarily more strongly than in the general population. Admittedly, there may be something about the Protestant tradition of the individual right to interpret Scripture, or the idea of the priesthood of all believers, which can come down to a very self-centred faith. But this strong individualism, enhanced by post-modernism, is prevalent in the Western culture at large.

So, in more general terms, is there, as the example we've just discussed seems to suggest, a certain lack of philosophical reflection on the part of some scientists that doesn't do justice to religion and actually ends up weakening their critique of faith?

It's a weakness of the British system; it may be equally true of North America. In the English-speaking world, the university system has been quite strongly divided; I went through seven years of university without a single lecture on the philosophy of science. Personally, I read it because of the people who were criticising my Christian faith, to find answers for myself. I was largely reading European writers, because they had done the work. Over here, we've produced scientists who have had no training in philosophy and who are not encouraged to reflect upon their own discipline.

What, then, did you take away from your studies of the philosophy of science?

Two things. One, the history of science – the things we've talked about regarding the under-girding of science by the Christian world-view; that was a great encouragement to me. The second thing was reading people like David Hume, Karl Popper and Michael Polanyi[23] to see how the philosophers had been critiquing the 'naïve' scientific method of Bacon and saying, 'Hold on! There are some big holes in it. It has worked, but let's justify its working in a rigorous philosophical way.'

If we're saying, 'This is the truth!' it's a sort of truth that hangs in the air without support, because its original support was a theological framework. So, is scientific truth more than what the scientific community of any one generation says it should be?

We've talked about intellectually motivated, religious criticism from secular scientists. What about the criticism from within Christianity's own ranks? Many biblical scholars and theologians have been heavily influenced by rationalism and the scientific method. Part of the Christian community itself seems to be struggling with 'what is written'!

Though I don't think the public is very aware of these internal discussions, except when something hits the headlines like the Gospel of Judas or the alleged discovery of Jesus' family tomb. Other disciplines like history were trying to become scientific, which impacted on biblical scholarship because, particularly in regard to the Hebrew Scriptures – the Old Testament – we're dealing with something that has some relation to history, the history of the nation of Israel. As a result, a mixture of techniques to study the text of the Bible was imported into biblical studies. Those techniques were increasingly based on rationalistic assumptions that came from the Enlightenment. In science, we have experiments; in scientific history, we have analogies. We look for analogous situations in different historic situations. We look for repeated events and, of course, a miracle by definition is not a repeatable event. So, when we claim that someone has risen from the dead, this is clearly not something that we observe repeatedly in human history. Therefore, when we have such miracles in a biblical story, the whole story becomes questionable.

The other issue is literary criticism. The basic technique of literary criticism, which derives from studying ancient texts, ought to be applied to the Bible. If we insist that everything in the first five books of the Bible was written by Moses, whereas literary criticism suggests that whoever put these texts together might have used earlier sources, we have a problem. Do we hang on to the tradition? Or do we re-examine our traditional understanding? And if we do the latter, what are the implications?

If we tie our understanding of inspiration to a very prophetic model – in other words, if we say, unless it was one particular person who sat down and wrote this under the inspiration of God, it's not inspired – then that doesn't fit when, for instance, we look at the book of Kings, where the writer tells us that they've gone and consulted the records, wherever they were, and that they've used sources. So, why should the writer of the books of Moses not have used existing sources? The outside world may see these issues not as a discussion but as a heated debate and a disagreement which is undermining the traditional understanding of the Bible.

Nonetheless, there is, undeniably, a divide between what we might call liberal and conservative, biblical scholarship, respectively; a divide which is caused largely by the degree to which scholars make science and reason the ultimate arbiter in their study of the Scriptures. We shall return to this question in more depth in the final chapter, as we consider the reliability of the Gospel record (see 'The Faith'). But now, let us turn to the first blow that the traditional, medieval world-view received from science and that still affects us today; for if philosopher Friedrich Nietzsche was right, modern astronomy, which began with Copernicus, has set humanity on a course from the centre of creation into a meaningless void.

1.

The Sky

Next time you get a chance to gaze at the night sky, take it. In your imagination, turn the clock back by a few thousand years. Picture yourself standing on a hill somewhere in the Mediterranean. The flickering lights above are retelling the Greek and Roman myths; stories of humans who have encountered the divine. There is *Hercules*, sprung from the loins of the father of the gods, set to fight *Leo*, who is crouching on the other side of the firmament. Next emerges fatal *Scorpio*, sent by a jealous goddess to sting the proud hunter *Orion*, who has quickly slipped behind the opposite horizon. Rising in the east is *lyra*, Orpheus' instrument, rescued by the gods – unlike its less fortunate owner – from the hands of the Furies, and suspended in the heavens to remind future generations of the prodigy singer. Meanwhile, ruddy Mars and radiant Venus trace the skies in planetary paths that are as hard to predict as war and love. The heavens tell you about struggling mortals and fickle deities. Life under the stars may be precarious, but it is still well defined within the clear-cut boundaries of land, water, and air.

Now move the clock forward to medieval times. Look up again. The stars have surrendered their divine authority. Placed there by the creator as tools for the human race to divide night and day, they circle the Earth, the centre of creation. The stars now bow to the one God, proclaiming his glory. You too are the work of his hands. Your life is encompassed by a finite, heavenly dome pointing you towards eternity.

By the sixteenth century, your perspective has changed once again. As you gaze at the stars, it dawns on you that they are much farther away than your forebears could ever have guessed.

You have a dizzying sense of rapidly decreasing in stature, while space expands to uncanny dimensions and the planet you call home drifts unstoppably from the centre. Cornered into seeming insignificance, you come face to face with the question of why you, the pinnacle of creation, would inhabit such average quarters.

By 1800, the night sky that once held the key to the divine and showed you your place in the world has not only reduced you and your planetary home to infinitesimal size, but it has lost much of its own former transcendence. You are witnessing little more than the movements of a machine. The sky is governed by mere natural laws of logic and reason. But at least you may hope that one day the world below might be as well.

If you look up this evening, the sky will tell you that the star that kept you warm during the day is one among 10^{24}. If you were able to move at the speed of light, you would need less than ten minutes to reach it, but a lifetime to approach one of its brighter sister stars above you that are located in the immediate cosmic neighbourhood. While there are hundreds of billions of galaxies in the observable part of the universe, it would take 2 million years of light-speed travel to reach even the closest one. In physical terms, you and the Earth on which you stand are immaterial. What, then, of human life? Can you honestly carry on believing it to be central, crucial, of universal significance? Or is it more likely to be a mere accidental, cosmic by-product? Have the stars stopped talking about meaning, destiny, and God?

Heaven Abolished?

Dr Lucas, I want to open this section with the key question: is belief in a personal God still tenable, given the size of the universe? In a sense, we're back to Richard Dawkins' criticism of Christians having a 'poky, little medieval view of the universe,' and, indeed, some people argue that we take ourselves far too seriously, given the immensity of the cosmos.

I've always found that a very strange conclusion to arrive at. If we believe in a creator at all, and the universe having produced personal beings that are self-conscious and able to interact with other people, I don't see how we can conclude that the creator can be anything other than a being that in some sense is personal. Not just a superhuman being; I think that's where some of the earlier religions went wrong. They made gods in the human image. What we are talking about is a personal being of a higher order of 'personalness' than we are, which is where I find that, to me, the Christian doctrine of the Trinity makes reasonable sense. If there is a God who is a transcendent being, God's personality is going to be of a higher order than ours. Not that we have three superhuman beings, but one being who is more complex than we are. And if there is a transcendent, infinite God, I see no logical problem with that infinite being having the ability to interact with finite creatures and, indeed, with an infinite number of them.

I think the difficulty arises because people still work with the idea of God being some sort of superhuman being who therefore is limited and cannot have an interest in such a big universe and, at the same time, take minor creatures in it seriously. I think it's a defect in people's understanding of the nature of God.

But what about another risk of misunderstanding; of religious people taking themselves and their daily affairs too seriously and carrying around with them their 'pocket-size' God, who will come in handy when they need him?

That is a fair criticism. Indeed, we have done this in the course of history. We demean other creatures, in our case the non-human creation, and make ourselves into little despots. That clearly is wrong and is, I think, contrary to Christian teaching. The other aspect of taking ourselves too seriously is to make God in our own image and to think that we must be able to order God around in some sort of way, so that God is always on our side if we are in disagreement with other people.

Going back to Copernicus' discovery that we are not the navel of the universe – how do we cope with that 'cosmological insult'?

Clearly that comes back to thinking in terms of importance being related to geographical position. That's something we all have a tendency to do. We'll think of, say, Rome or London as the centre of the world. And we think of the planet as the centre of the cosmos, so it has to be at the geographical centre. But, of course, importance doesn't equate necessarily with geographical position or with physical size. There are other ways of judging importance. Clearly when I held my first child in my arms and he weighed only a few pounds – I can't remember exactly how many . . .

Your wife would!

No doubt! Anyway, he only weighed a few pounds and was small in size, but to me he was one of the most important beings in the world. It had nothing to do with size, but with personal relationship. This is how the Christian faith understands our importance in a relationship with God. It's God's personal interest in us, not because we deserve it intrinsically, but because God is a God of love.

Interestingly, long before people knew about the size of the universe, Israel's King David said, 'what is man that you are mindful of him . . .?' (Ps. 8:4, NIV)

Yes, we all have these moments of awe, an awareness of our own insignificance and our unworthiness, which is another aspect of the Judeo-Christian tradition which emphasises the holiness of God. So we do have that sense of reverence which acts as a check on our own arrogance.

How do you deal with these questions when you discuss them with your students; for example, when you touch on the aforementioned play by Brecht, Life of Galileo, which draws that very conclusion, that heaven has been abolished and that we are no longer the pinnacle of creation?

I don't think that really applies to our own students at Bristol Baptist College, because they're already used to thinking of human significance in terms of relationship with God. Certainly my wife finds, in teaching science in secondary school, that the module on space physics raises the issue of the size of the universe and our own seeming insignificance, and this does come up in discussions in class. But that is because the students are working within a framework that thinks in purely materialistic terms. If the material universe is all there is and if we're such a tiny bit of matter, how can we be important? My wife then often uses the example of the little child or a student's brother or sister, and that significance can be thought of in quite a different way, which can be an eye-opener, because they haven't made that shift of paradigm. That may also be to do with the fact that we live in a society in which relationships have been much devalued and importance is measured in terms of material things.

What if we – the supposed pinnacle of creation – were not only physically minute but not unique either? What if the universe were teeming with civilisations? Would that pose a problem for Christian theology or any theistic religion?

I don't think so. In fact, long before the Space Age, Thomas Aquinas discussed this back in the thirteenth century. In some sense, we go back to an early Christian understanding that there would be almost more of a problem if there weren't any other civilisations. When theologians have debated the question of why God created the world, the most satisfactory answer, it is generally agreed, is that it is an overflow of God's love. God is a creative being in the first place and, secondly, God is love, and it is the nature of love to want to shower itself upon other creatures. In that sense we might expect God to create a universe where there are more, rather than fewer, creatures with whom he could have a love relationship, and therefore why limit creation to one planet in one solar system?

The unfathomable size of the universe may lead some people to abandon belief in a personal God who cares about, let alone for, human beings. On the other hand, there are scientists such as the late Fred Hoyle,[1] who said that nothing shook his atheism as much as the discovery of the fine-tuning of the universe, without which there would be no life. Are there hints of a creator in the cosmos?

There is something about the nature of the universe and its fundamental constants that shows us that this is a universe that is finely tuned to produce carbon-based life. The nature of the laws and the relative strength of the fundamental forces[2] are very finely balanced; sometimes the numbers that are used to express the balance are one divided by ten to the power of fifty or so, and it wouldn't be possible to have carbon-based life in the universe without that sort of fine-tuning. That has led Hoyle to say the universe is a put-up job, or Paul Davis[3] to suggest that there must be some sort of mind behind the universe, although he wouldn't call it a personal God.

People have spoken of an 'intelligent big bang' . . .

Yes, exactly. I would see this as a pointer; it does raise a question. But to answer the question, 'Why does the universe have this nature?', we would have to go outside the universe, as it were; we would have to move into metaphysics. Essentially, we have three options. One is to say there is a creator God of some sort, with the emphasis being put on the rationality and power of that being. Second, we can do what many cosmologists do and favour what is called the 'many world hypothesis', which suggests that there might be literally millions of universes, each with their own sets of physical laws; and given that big number of universes, one of them may well come up with life.

Is there any evidence for that kind of 'multiverse'?

It's speculation. We're in the universe that we can observe because it's the kind of universe that would produce us, but we can't step outside it. We might say it's not totally unscientific. Some of the speculation of what might be the origin of the big bang might lead us to say that this is not the only big bang that could happen. So there could be many other big bangs and many other universes. But strictly speaking, this is a metaphysical hypothesis, because it goes beyond anything we could ever observe or verify by scientific means. So it's going beyond science, and in one sense we might say it is a less satisfactory hypothesis, because it still leaves us asking, 'Why are there many universes? Why is there not nothing?' We might say there's one universe that is fit for life because it is one in many millions –

someone has to win the lottery sometime. But there is still the question, 'Why is there a multiverse?'

And the third option?

The third option is to shrug our shoulders and say, 'We don't know. It just happened. But metaphysics is illegitimate because we have to stick with what we can see.'

I think in this context it's important to point out that for life to 'just happen' it takes more than a few chemicals and couple of lightning bolts.

Yes, a lot of cosmologists as well as bio-chemists talk very glibly about a primitive soup. Just put the right chemicals together and it'll all happen. At the moment we don't have more than very small glimmerings of how biologically important molecules might have come into being. It wouldn't surprise me if, say, in a few centuries time, we do understand it. In some ways I'd expect that. But so far, we don't have any particularly convincing ideas of how life originated from inorganic chemicals. Coming at it from my Christian angle, I would say that the amazing thing is that matter has the unique properties it does, and that the laws of the cosmos are such that they are capable of producing carbon-based life. It wouldn't surprise me if one day we could unravel the whole story – from chemicals to humans – but that would not in any way diminish my understanding of God.

Does that tie in with what you said earlier about importance not being the same as physical size?

Yes. As far as we know, the most complex being in the whole universe is the living cell. Stars can be understood with first year university level particle physics, thermo-dynamics and gas laws, whereas the human cell is still something that boggles our minds.

The most popular model of how it all began is the big bang theory. What does it say in broad terms?

It touches on quantum physics. First, we have an energy field. To use a simple visualisation, if we think of a magnet, and we sprinkle some iron filings, they form a pattern that shows us there's an (in this case, magnetic) energy field. Another energy field we're all familiar with is gravity. Now, quantum theory predicts that if we have an energy field, while the average energy over the field is zero, the energy at any given point can fluctuate into positive and negative energy. Think of the sea, which is level – we talk about sea level – and the waves that come and go as the fluctuations. Big bang cosmology says that we can get a fluctuation such that, out of this energy field, it produces a cosmos. This is why we can think in terms of many big bangs; we could have them in all sorts of places, out of the energy field. But that does suggest that the universe has a beginning, a fluctuation in a quantum vacuum, as it's called – not a vacuum in our traditional sense of there being nothing there, but there being an energy field of an average zero. When the big bang theory came up, it was doing battle with Fred Hoyle's theory about the cosmos, which was rather different: the so-called 'steady state' cosmos, which says that there has always been a universe, although it is expanding. An expanding universe is the basis of the big bang theory; since the 1920s, we have known that the other galaxies are moving away from ours. Hoyle's explanation of an expanding universe that always existed was to say that as it expands, new matter comes into being all the time; so the average space between the galaxies remains the same because new galaxies are produced. Many people said, 'Well, that's a totally non-Christian theory because there is no beginning'; and that's why, as an atheist, Fred Hoyle liked it. If there's no beginning, we don't need a creator. That said, we still have the question – why is there an expanding universe?

But whereas big bang cosmology seemed to say that 13 billion years ago the universe began, and a beginning fitted with Christian theology of creation, it doesn't really get to the heart of the matter. The important point about Christian theology is the answer to the question 'Why is there anything in the first place?' – because God created it!

It is worth remembering that long before the arrival of quantum physics, in the early centuries of the church, Christians were also doing battle with competing cosmologies.

One of those world-views was that of the Stoics. In Stoic philosophy there was no distinction between God and the world. The universe was the body and God was the spirit that animates it; we can't separate the two. God and the world is one and the same thing. Christians insisted that this was not the biblical view and that the creator was transcendent and separate from the universe. We talk about a universe created outside God, creation out of nothing. There was no world before there was God, and when God created the world, God didn't use pre-existing matter.

The other competing world-view was one that, I suppose, had its roots in Platonic philosophy. This is the view that there always has been matter and there has always been God. So, matter is eternal and God is eternal, and creation is a case of God fashioning something out of existing matter. But Christians said that God had created matter outside of himself and from nothing.

Once modern science developed, the question was transferred from this purely philosophical question – how God relates to the world – to the more physical question: How and why did the world begin? Therefore, in twentieth-century cosmology, we get Christians taking sides and saying that the big bang is more Christian than the 'steady state' universe theory; but neither is more or less Christian than the other. God could create a 'steady state' universe and, once it had been produced, from living within it, we would see no beginning. Then again, God could also have created the universe by a big bang. Within the traditional big bang model, we can work our way back by 13 billion years. Stephen Hawking[4] said that we can write the equations for a big bang cosmology in such a way that it doesn't appear to have a beginning in time and therefore we can't specify a beginning – what he calls a 'closed surface' universe. And, as a Christian I can say, yes, God could create that sort of universe; an expanding universe that, looked at in one way, had a beginning in time, but if we look at it another way – Stephen Hawking's way – we can't specify where it began in time. Many cosmologists are not convinced by Hawking, but that's a debate between the cosmologists. It doesn't make any difference theologically.

Seeing as, from what you're saying, cosmology – the theory of the ori-
gin and nature of the universe – is both complex and speculative, it
seems tempting to return to the argument that there must be an ulti-
mate, divine, mystery about the world we live in; that there are gaps in
our knowledge that only God can close.

Well, it goes back to Newton saying, 'I can't understand the universe according to the law of gravity alone. Why is the solar system stable? There are five planets (those that were known in
Newton's day), and though the sun is by far the largest body, the
planets are sufficiently massive to interact with one another and
therefore the system ought to be pulled out of kilter. So God must
be doing something periodically to prevent it from falling apart.'
Initially he seems to have thought of a direct intervention of God,
and then he had a brilliant, second thought – brilliant in his mind
– which was that maybe comets were God's mechanism. People
had realised that comets had highly elliptical, even hyperbolical
orbits and Newton figured that the comets might be exerting the
type of gravitational pull when they entered and left the solar system that corrected the imbalances. For a while people thought that
was quite a nifty mechanism. They didn't know that the gravitational force of comets isn't all that great because they are not much
more than dirty snowballs.

The God of the gaps became quite a popular argument and it
got transposed into all sorts of other forms. In biology, say, people looked at complex things like the human eye and said this
was too complex to have come about by chance; God must have
made it.

Is there some resonance here with the Christian belief in miracles?

Well, we do believe that the creator is someone who is not shut
out of his universe, as deists argue. The biblical witness is that
God is concerned about his universe and interacts with it occa-
sionally via what we call miracles. So, there is some sort of theological sense to the argument. But others argued that if we believe
in an infinite creator, surely he would be able to create a seamless
system without gaps, a world that would not fall apart. Leibniz[5]
disagreed with Newton and, in a letter written to Caroline,

Princess of Wales, in November 1715, he accused him of presenting God as an incompetent creator.

So Christians were divided over this from the start. On a popular level, the God of the gaps argument caught people's imagination. But over time, more and more gaps have closed and people have felt that God is being pushed out of the universe and that maybe indeed God isn't there at all. Darwin's theory of evolution seemed to give the God of the gaps another hefty shove and Hawking thinks the same is true of his version of the big bang theory. But all this hinges on the same type of understanding of God's interaction with creation. I like the quotation from Professor Charles Coulson, who, when I was an undergraduate at Oxford, was a professor of applied mathematics at Oxford. I think he was the person who invented the term 'God of the gaps'. He said that when we come across a gap in our science our reaction should not be to say, 'God is there' but to become better scientists and seek to fill the gap. I agree with that.

What about the fact that we are the species that is seeking to fill the gaps? Does that not take us back to the 'divine image'?

There's a saying attributed to Einstein that the only thing that is incomprehensible about the universe is that it is comprehensible. And indeed it is mind-boggling that we should be able to understand the universe at all. This is particularly true if we think in terms of mathematics. If we try and explain the human ability to understand maths purely on 'survival of the fittest' terms, one would understand why we have a basic understanding of arithmetic – because it's helpful to know that you have two children and three chickens to feed them, or you are a group of a dozen humans and you're being opposed by a group of twenty, so it's not worth fighting – that sort of thing. As for geometry, it's helpful to know how to make a right angle to prevent walls from collapsing on you. But when we get to the higher realms of mathematics it becomes amazing that the human mind can understand it. For example, in the middle of the nineteenth century someone came up with something called tensor calculus that seemed a mathematical game without any practical relevance at all. But when Einstein was trying to generalise his special theory of relativity as a description of space in time, he was having great problems until someone asked him whether he had thought of using tensor calculus. He hadn't, because it was regarded purely as a mathematician's game. But when he explored it, he found that it was exactly what he needed to express his theory of general relativity. So it is quite amazing that something that has come out of the human mind should be exactly what is needed to explain the nature of space-time – scientists would say, to explain the nature of reality. Why should this happen? Could this indicate that we are made in the image of the creator?

There are other phenomena that characterise humans, such as music, that are hard to explain in evolutionary terms. OK, singing may go back to primeval mating calls, but what of Beethoven's Great Fugue?

I agree; certainly the more esoteric forms of aesthetics become very difficult to understand in pure survival terms.

Adam and Astronomy

Now, when we look at the age of the universe – roughly 13 billion years – and the biblical witness; how shall the two ever meet?

The bridge is in the area of interpreting the Bible. The question is what sort of literature we've got, particularly in the opening chapters of Genesis. We've talked about revelation and I think we need to take very seriously the way that God's revelation has been given. Throughout the Bible it always comes in 'incarnate' form – God's Word expressed in human words. Christians would say that is supremely evidenced in Jesus. God becomes a human being; that's what incarnation means. 'And the Word was made flesh' (Jn. 1:14, KJV). So the highest form of divine revelation is in a human being, which again is the most complex form we can understand. But throughout biblical history, God's revelation comes in an incarnated form and has to be understood in its historical and cultural context. Jesus was a particular person who spoke a particular language in a particular culture at a particular time in history. And if we are to understand Jesus' teaching, we have to understand it in the terms of a first-century Jew speaking Aramaic, whose words have been conveyed to us in Greek. We can't understand Jesus' sayings fully unless we understand the context as best we can. That's true of the whole of the Bible. The prophets of the Old Testament spoke in Hebrew, lived at certain times; and the biblical revelation is expressed in the kinds of literature that were around in that particular culture.

In other words, we mustn't assume the forms of literature that we are familiar with in our Western culture.

No. For instance, in Mesopotamian narratives of their kings' military campaigns, events were often described in one geographical location and then in another, even though in the first description they may have recorded several incidents that were spread out over time but all happened in that place. Then they would move on to describe what happened in the next place. We, on the other hand, arrange our material according to a time flow. In Mesopotamia they would organise it geographically. If we don't understand that, we have great difficulty in working out what happened. And there may be places in the Old Testament where the same sort of principle is applied.

When we come to the early chapters of Genesis, we have to take into account that they are written in the way that people in the Ancient Near East would write about the beginning of the world. They're not asking modern, scientific questions; they're asking questions about meaning and the nature of things more in a moral than a physical sense. And that's the primary emphasis of the opening chapters of the Bible. If we look at chapter 1 of Genesis, we're likely to go 'Oh! That's interesting; sun and moon aren't created till day four. But there are three days beforehand with mornings and evenings; so what's going on here?' I would suggest – and this is not my idea but one that goes back to the early Christian centuries – that, clearly, this isn't meant to be a chronological account. The headline is 'In the beginning God created the heavens and the earth . . . [and] the earth was formless and empty' (Gen. 1:1,2, NIV). And God spends the first three days shaping the earth by separating light from darkness, waters above the firmament from those below the firmament, the land from the water and, having finished that, he then spends three days filling the shapes. So, where there is light and dark, he makes sun, moon and stars. Where there are waters above the firmament and below the firmament, he creates birds and flying animals and creatures that live in the waters. And where there is land and water, he creates land and water animals. So this is not a chronological account but one that says 'This is a carefully ordered and structured and thought-out creation'. In the Near Eastern context this was very important, because the general view was that everything started with chaos and a big battle between the forces of chaos and the creator god, who had to give order to creation. And the big question was, how stable was that order? Might it all collapse into chaos again? The biblical story, on the other hand, is saying, 'No chaotic forces, no big battle but a well-ordered, planned creation which is stable.' That's what Genesis is trying to convey.

In terms of timing – when creation happened – Archbishop Usher worked his way through the genealogies in Genesis 1–11 and then in Chronicles and Matthew; the problem with that is, it assumes an understanding of numbers in genealogies which is very much a scientific, Enlightenment understanding. It is worth comparing the biblical genealogies to the Sumerian king lists. The Sumerians lived in Mesopotamia in the third and fourth milleniums BC. They invented writing and passed much of their culture on to the Assyrians and Babylonians. In the Sumerian king lists, as in the biblical genealogies, there is a big dividing line of kings that lived before the flood and after the flood. The list names several kings that ruled between creation and the flood. In Genesis we have creation, then ten patriarchs, then the flood and, after that, more patriarchs. In the Sumerian version, the kings before the flood live a lot longer than those after the flood. And the pattern is similar with the biblical patriarchs. One of the kings who lived after the flood, according to the Sumerian king list, is called En-Mebaragisi. He is known to have been a real person, because there are inscriptions about him and there is archaeological evidence. The inscriptions show that he had a quite normal length of reign, a few decades, but in the king list he reigned for 900 years. (The reigns before the flood are given as over ten thousand years, so in comparison his was a short reign.) So the pattern of the reigns before the flood being much longer than after is saying that life was a lot better before the flood and that, since the flood, things have been going downhill. All this shows that the numbers in the king list are not the actual lengths of the reigns but are being used symbolically. Therefore, we can't add them up to give a chronological time span. That's where Usher was led astray, by treating the numbers as we would in our modern understanding.

What would you answer someone who countered that, if the Bible were as inaccurate as in your example, it couldn't be trusted at all; so you must be wrong in reading the creation story and the genealogies symbolically?

The ironic thing is that this kind of approach buys into the Enlightenment view that scientific truth is the only reliable truth there is and, therefore, if the Bible is supposed to be reliable, it has to be scientifically true. We are accepting the assumption that scientific truth is the only sort of truth; therefore we've got to question all other sorts of truth – not just the Bible, but any kind of experience that cannot be validated in a scientific kind of way. This ignores the fact that there are numerous ways in which we express truth. For instance, the deep theological and moral truth of the story of the Good Samaritan doesn't depend on whether Jesus quoted a newspaper report on an event that had really happened on the way to Jericho the previous week. Anyone reading that story in any culture can recognise the moral point and the theological point, i.e. that my neighbour is anyone who is in desperate need. Unless we recognise the relationship between Jews and Samaritans, the culture of the time and the deep animosity between the two, we miss just how revolutionary the story told by Jesus is. But the main point – help those who need help – still gets across. A great deal of what we express as truth happens in what we might call figurative language. We often use metaphors and comparisons, which are totally untrue if we take them literally, but are true if we see the point of the comparison. Jesus says that it's harder for a rich man to get into heaven than for a camel to go through the eye of a needle (Mt. 19:24), so people in the Middle Ages came up with the idea that there must have been a small gate in the city walls of Jerusalem called the Eye of a

Needle. But there's no evidence that there ever was such a gate. Jesus is just making an absurd comparison and that's the whole point. It's just as absurd to believe that someone who hangs onto their riches and makes them their god will enter heaven.

So, the religious and the secular literalist fall into the same trap. I'm reminded of Yuri Gagarin[6] saying that he hadn't seen God during his space voyage, therefore God didn't exist.

We need to distinguish between how people visualise things and how they understand things. Going back to the Old Testament, the writers worked with a three-storey universe: the underworld – Sheol – the Earth on which we live, and the heavens above the firmament, where God is. But then King Solomon says in his prayer that neither the temple he has built nor the heavens can contain God (1 Kgs. 8:27). So, although we may think of God living in some location up there, really God is so big that we can't limit him to that. It's just a picture, and we realise it's a limited picture. We have to think in picture language about God and the non-material world; the problems arise when we begin to take the pictures literally.

In the story of the ascension, a cloud comes down and Jesus disappears into the cloud. Throughout the Old Testament some appearances of God happen in connection with a cloud. Despite the fact that in some Christian art the ascension is depicted as Jesus going up like a space rocket, as it were, with his feet dangling from a cloud, that is not the picture in the account as found in the book of Acts. A cloud comes and Jesus disappears into it; this is much more like someone moving from one space-time dimension into another, rather than the space-rocket model. So, we're not encouraged to think of heaven as 'up there', but as 'somewhere else'. The biblical imagery is about heaven as where God is; a different reality, and not a different location in this reality. The imagery of the cloud is taken from a wider, Near Eastern way of thinking about the gods. The god Baal rides on the clouds. The realm of the gods is a mysterious place, sometimes visualised as 'out there', or 'up there'.

The question, then, is: Where do you draw the line between recognising metaphorical language, while also taking, say, the resurrection or ascension literally as historical events?

We have to judge, first of all, by the nature of the literature that we're reading – as with the first chapter of Genesis, which, I think, is an extended metaphor. God is presented as a worker doing a week's work and his artefact is the cosmos. It's different with the resurrection and ascension accounts. At least I don't, and many scholars don't, have a sense of moving into an extended metaphorical, symbolical language, but these are texts talking in terms of real-life experience. These women go to a tomb expecting to find a dead body to be embalmed and they expect a big stone that will need to be rolled away, and that's not what they find. OK, they have a vision of angels; however, that's not moving into the realm of myth, but the realm of supernatural experience, if you like, which people have had down through the ages. Similarly, when we read the account of the ascension, the apostles have a notion that the period following the resurrection where they experienced Jesus in some kind of bodily form is brought to an end by the ascension. Regarding the symbolism of the cloud which, in the Old Testament, is used to talk about experiences of God, we could say there's a sort of psychological experience here that is hard to evaluate. But we can also say, behind this is a real experience of God coming and going with the imagery of the cloud.

2.

The Cell

Our next chapter starts on board the Beagle, the vessel that carried Charles Darwin to the Galapagos Islands and Tierra del Fuego, where, as he would note later, 'certain facts in the distribution of . . . organic beings . . . seemed to throw some light on the origin of species'.[1] That which started out as a biological theory rapidly evolved into a philosophical challenge of Copernican proportions. Christianity, still a major spiritual and social force in Darwin's day, claimed that humans had been made by God, and that they were the pinnacle of his creation and core object of his attention. Evolution, however, appeared to undermine both ideas. Firstly, as for God: Was he a necessary, even probable, agent given that random biological processes seemed perfectly able to do the job, and a benevolent Father in heaven seemed hard to spot amidst the ruthless competition and wastage of life that fuelled evolution? Secondly, as for humanity: Could we still claim to be doing more than enacting one among countless episodes in evolution's book – mere animals descended from primitive life forms that one day would make way for more complex, better-adapted ones?

Darwin's theory challenged Christians who sought to maintain face-value readings of the Scriptures, as well as those who took a more metaphorical view. Not only did the book of Genesis speak of six days of creation while evolution presupposed billions of years but more importantly, Genesis postulated divine intervention and purpose, while all evolution seemed to require was biology and chance. How did all this relate to the age-old question of who we are, where we come from, and how we are meant to live?

Evolved?

Dr Lucas, when people nowadays talk about the origin of the diversity of life forms as we know it, they usually refer to evolution, and evolution is inextricably linked with the name of Charles Darwin. But is there such a thing as pre-Darwinism?

Darwin wasn't the first to have the idea of evolution if we think of it in terms of organisms gradually changing from one form into another. That idea was around in the sixth century BC among the so-called Ionian philosophers. But great towering figures of Greek philosophy had different views. Aristotle claimed that species were fixed and that the ladder of being, from the simplest to the most complex, didn't change. That idea dominated right down to the eighteenth century. But then we do get people thinking again in terms of evolution – Buffon and Lamarck,[2] and Erasmus Darwin, Charles' grandfather, who had the idea that species change into one another. But when, just after Christmas 1831, Darwin boarded the *Beagle* as a naturalist for a voyage which was going to explore particularly the coast of Latin America, he (as far as we can gather) still believed in fixed species. He had read Paley's[3] book, *Natural Theology or Evidences of the Existence and Attributes of the Deity*, published in 1802, on the evidences of design, which was widely read in the early nineteenth century, and he was very impressed by it. He spent nearly five years on the ship and returned in October 1836. During that period he collected a vast amount of data about flora and fauna, but he was equally interested in geology. He took with him a book by Charles Lyell,[4] *Principles of Geology*, which had just been published when he left on the Beagle. Lyell argued the case that the present geological form of the Earth was the result of gradual change involving the forces that we observe today – volcanoes, erosion, earthquakes and so on.

What was it about the Galapagos Islands that appeared to contribute so much to Darwin's theory?

It was the observing of finches, which had all sorts of different kinds of habitats and had adapted to them. Some were nut-eaters; some were similar to woodpeckers, and so on. That doesn't seem to have struck him while he was there; he was too busy collecting. But he began to realise that there were certain phenomena that might need some sort of explanation. The finches were very similar to those he had seen on the mainland; so how had they adapted to different habitats in different parts of the islands? The thought that they had come from the mainland and adapted to their new surroundings seemed more likely to him than different kinds having been created in the beginning. The same kind of thing applied to other creatures on the Galapagos Islands – tortoises, lizards, mockingbirds.

You mentioned Lyell. He also read Malthus[5] – not himself a biologist but nonetheless influential for Darwin's theory.

When he got back in 1836, as far as we can see, he was no doubt beginning to rethink, but he had no formed ideas and he says in his autobiography that one of the crucial helps in his thinking was a book he read in 1838 by Malthus, *Essay on the Principle of Population*, in which the author grappled with the issue that the population grows at a vastly faster rate than the supply of food. There is therefore a struggle for existence; disease and war result from this and keep the population in line with resources. That caused something to click in Darwin's mind. He had been struggling to account for the same observation in the animal world: population growth and decline while natural resources are limited. So what was going on in nature was the struggle for existence. Darwin had also been struck by variations in the forms of creatures that he had seen throughout the world. But how would these variations happen? Well, Malthus gave him the idea – the competition for resources.

From as early as 1838, Darwin was trying to work out how evolution could happen. He wrote an extensive essay on this in 1844 and circulated it among his fellow-scientific friends for comments and criticism. But he didn't publish it for another fourteen years.

Was that the first draft of The Origin of Species?

It's the essence, but *The Origin of Species* is a lot longer. What prompted him in the end to publish was that in 1858 another naturalist, Alfred Russell Wallace, who had worked in the Amazon basin and the Far East and puzzled over the same issues as Darwin because he had seen the same variety of creatures, came up with the same answer: the struggle for existence. And in the space of a few days, Wallace wrote a paper on this which he sent to Darwin to ask for his comment and assistance in getting it published. That caused Darwin a great dilemma, because Wallace had arrived at the same conclusion. Darwin's friends knew he had had the idea fourteen years earlier and suggested that Darwin's work and Wallace's paper should be read together at a meeting of the Linnaean Society, which was the leading biological academic society of the day. And that's what happened. But it didn't excite any great furore at the time. It did, however, prompt Darwin to publish his Origin of Species, which sold out in a day or two and then went into several editions over the following decades.

Why did Darwin wait fourteen years between the initial essay and the book?

Some think he was afraid of opposition. But it wasn't primarily opposition from the church, though I think he was concerned about religious responses to the book. In 1844 another book called *The Vestiges of Creation* was brought out anonymously by a Scottish publisher and amateur scientist called Robert Chambers. He expounded a kind of evolution but it was a very poor book from a scientific point of view and it got panned by all the scientists of the day as well as raising a certain amount of mockery among the general public. As a result, Darwin felt he had to make sure that his book would be better argued to avoid the same kind of hostile reception. He seems to have been quite a perfectionist and that was almost certainly a factor in it taking him so long. He was also involved in other studies, like that of barnacles, which diverted him. And he suffered from ill health.

Let's return to Paley's book on divine design, which was very influential in Darwin's day, and his famous watchmaker analogy; in what sense did it turn out to be flawed?

Paley said, suppose he was walking across heath land and kicked against something and looked down and it was a stone; there would be nothing remarkable. But if he bent down and found what he had kicked against was a watch, and picked it up and opened the back and saw the cogwheels all meshing together – even if he had never seen a watch before, he would recognise that this was something that had been designed by someone and that it was a mechanism that couldn't just have occurred by chance. Paley applied this to the natural world, particularly that of creatures. One of his examples was the human eye – so nicely adapted, with a lens and so on. It wasn't a new argument; it goes back to the Greeks. It's used in the Middle Ages by Thomas Aquinas as one of his five arguments for the existence of God. But it had been strongly criticised by the Scottish philosopher David Hume in the eighteenth century, before Paley. Hume had asked why, when we look at the natural world, we could not conclude that it is a kind of divine organism without an external creator – which amounts to a pantheistic rather than a Christian view of the world. Hume also questioned how we measure design. How do we know when something is designed and when it isn't? To use a simple example, in the Lake District we can find very nicely balanced rocks, because the lower, softer layer has been eroded and the upper, harder layer has been left; so we have a rock balanced on a tiny pinnacle. Now, we might conclude that a person had designed that by carving the rock, when in fact it has come about by erosion. So Hume was arguing the question, how do we decide whether something has been designed or come about in a natural way? We only know this world, and though it looks designed to us, how do we know that it is, if we can't compare it to other worlds?

And finally, Paley's model was undermined by Darwin's theory, not via philosophical argument, but biological findings.

Yes. Darwin was saying that creatures are not so finely adapted because of an external designer but because of the pressures of natural selection.

At what point did this become a religious issue?

People were, first of all, debating evolution as a scientific idea. They were divided because those who opposed it said they couldn't see a viable mechanism, that is, how evolution could happen. But then it was also seen as a moral and philosophical question. Human rights and human freedom had been major issues in the French Revolution and during the revolutions of 1848;[6] but if humans had come into being from some animal origin, what was special about them? If humans were just another animal, how can we talk, say, about freedom of the will?

As for the religious argument: a lot had been invested in the argument of design as a way of proving the existence of God. The whole of what was called natural theology had developed as a way of learning about God by looking at the world. Some people saw this as a way of preparing people for the Christian message of the gospel by saying, 'Look at the world; isn't it reasonable to believe in a creator God?' And Darwin seemed to be undercutting that.

But, as you said, the reaction to Darwin, both from the religious and the scientific corners, was very mixed.

Yes, there were still many scientists who weren't convinced by his argument. In the first edition of *The Origin of Species* (1859), he included one chapter on objections to the theory; by the time he had got to the sixth edition, there were two chapters on objections. So he was well aware of the scientific weaknesses, and that what he was presenting was a probable idea, but he had not been able to prove it conclusively.

There were others who objected for moral or religious reasons. But there were also quite a few Christian theologians who were reasonably convinced scientifically and felt that the moral and theological objections could be overcome. So the response was mixed, and the picture we get in retrospect is somewhat affected by the spin that was put on it by some of Darwin's followers, such as Thomas Huxley,[7] because they made something of a crusade out of the issue.

Huxley is perhaps best remembered for his controversy with the Bishop of Oxford, Samuel Wilberforce. Did Huxley win the argument on the grounds of science or of rhetoric?

Wilberforce attacked Darwin's ideas, primarily as a representative not of the church but of the objecting scientists. At that time, a lot of scientists were still clergy, because they had the education and some of them at least had the time to invest in scientific work. Wilberforce had done his homework. He had been briefed by the objecting scientists he represented and he lost the argument not on the science but on the rhetoric. The story goes that at the end of his speech he turned to Huxley and said, 'From which side are you descended; from an ape on your grandfather's side or your grandmother's side?' Huxley replied that he'd rather be descended from an ape than be related to someone who made such remarks. At the time the debate didn't make the national news and it wasn't until Francis Darwin wrote about it in his biography of his father that it became part of the mythology about the debate.

Huxley described himself as an agnostic. Was that because of Darwin's theory?

Huxley, as far as we know, was a sceptic of religion before Darwin published *The Origin of Species*. And in fact Huxley wasn't totally convinced by the book. He readily embraced the idea of natural selection but he didn't seem to believe that it solved the whole problem. The issue was: where does variation come from, and how is it passed on from one generation to the next?

He didn't know genetics.

And it took another fifty years till people had an answer to the question. Huxley's real interest seems to have been with Darwin's methodology – looking for natural causes. He saw this as a refining of the scientific method and its first serious application to the world of biology. He used Darwin as his tool to forward the prestige of science in late Victorian Britain. He invented the word 'agnostic'. This may have been to do with the demise of the argument of design. In a sense, Huxley was a religious man, but it was a kind of nature religion, which had been around particularly among German philosophers in the early nineteenth century. Huxley talked about the 'church scientific', by which he meant the community of natural philosophers. He talked about being a 'priest of nature'. He held Sunday schools, which were classes in elementary science and in which people sang hymns to nature. So he tried to establish a parallel religious movement.

What about Darwin's faith?

Darwin seems to have gradually drifted away from orthodox Christianity. Probably at the heart of his loss of faith is the problem of suffering, which may have come to the fore mainly through his own personal experience. He was deeply affected by the death of his daughter Annie; the death of that innocent young child may have hit him harder than anything else and made him sensitive to the problem of suffering. In his later writings he talks about the suffering of creatures in the process of natural selection; he found that difficult to square with the concept of a God who is all-powerful and all-good. Darwin's scientific work did exacerbate the problem for him. At the end of *The Origin of Species*, he is still prepared to talk about a creator; in his later writings to his friends, he seems to have veered towards agnosticism. He couldn't square Christian faith with what he saw in the world and ended up saying, 'I just don't know.'

Let's return to the scientific debate. Why did many scientists reject Darwin's theory of evolution?

One major issue was the question of mechanism, how variation is passed on. The ironic thing is that, around 1860, Gregor Mendel,[8] in Austria, did his work on breeding peas, which led him to the conclusion that there are specific units of inheritance – what we now call genes – which are passed on from parent to child. The problem Darwin had was that of dilution. Suppose a giraffe was born with a slightly longer neck. It might have an advantage of survival, because it could reach leaves in trees that other giraffes couldn't. It would have a better diet, be healthier and produce more offspring. Now the problem is that the giraffe would mate with an average giraffe. So, if its neck is, say, 10 cms longer and it mates with a normal giraffe, does this mean that their offspring's necks will be 5 cms longer than normal? And once they mate with average giraffes, will the neck length only be 2.5 cms above average? So the variation would disappear over time, rather than being passed on. That was the criticism of Darwin's model, and he had no real answer; nor did anyone else, until Gregor Mendel's work was rediscovered in the early 1900s. Unfortunately, Mendel had published his findings in a fairly obscure scientific journal and very few people seem to have read it. And if they did, they didn't spot its significance.

Going back to our long-necked giraffe . . .

Mendel discovered that there are units of inheritance that can be passed on. So the giraffe with the slightly longer neck would be born with that neck because a slight mutation had taken place in the unit of inheritance – the gene – which governs neck length. And the giraffe would then pass that mutated gene on to its offspring. The idea of the survival of the fittest would mean that the giraffes with the longer necks would get the best leaves, be healthier, have more offspring and gradually there would be more and more giraffes with longer necks. That was the answer to Darwin's problem of the mechanism of variation.

You said Darwin ended up filling two book chapters with responses to criticism. Evidently, there were several issues.

One was the fossil record. What struck him while he was in Latin America was that not only do we get a balance of similarity and difference between creatures living in different habitats – the Galapagos finches being a prime example – but we also have a balance of similarity and difference between fossil creatures and creatures alive today. As he met animals like the sloth or the armadillo for the first time, he also discovered fossil sloth and armadillos, which were somewhat different from the living ones. So why, if we think of all species being fixed as created by God, do we have armadillos and sloth that don't exist today, that presumably were fitted to their habitats long ago, whereas now we have somewhat different specimens? For Darwin, the idea of descent with variation and natural selection was the answer. But the problem was, the fossil record didn't give him a nice, continuous history. There were missing links, and scientists jumped on that pretty early. Part of that missing link terminology goes back to Aristotle's idea of the ladder of being. And that ladder ought to be complete.

Darwin's answer to the missing links was two-fold. First of all, fossilisation only occurs in very special circumstances. Many creatures are eaten by others or their skeletons are blown to the wind. Bodies only rarely get naturally buried in a way that they aren't eaten by microbes and are preserved and turned to stone, which produces the fossils. Secondly, Darwin argued that people hadn't been looking for fossils systematically for more than a hundred or so years. Geology and palaeontology were very young sciences. Indeed, today the fossil record is more complete than in Darwin's day – and we've found nothing in the fossil record that contradicts his theory. Rather, we are beginning to fill some of the gaps.

What about the age of the Earth?

That was Darwin's third big problem – after the mechanism of variation and the missing links in the fossil record. He was well aware that evolution would take a very long time. And the problem for him was how we could measure the age of the Earth. Looking at the findings of geology of his day he guessed that the Earth must be tens or hundreds of millions of years old. Unfortunately for him, Lord Kelvin, who was probably the leading physicist in Britain at the time, decided to test the age of the Earth scientifically in the laboratory. He assumed – an idea going back to Pierre de Laplace – that the Earth had started as a ball of molten rock and cooled down. So he measured how long it took molten rock to cool down and on that basis he estimated that the Earth might be a million years old. That was far too short for Darwin's evolutionary process to work.

Whereas with today's estimated 4.5 billion or so years – problem solved! Going back to the implications Darwin's theory had for our ancestry; at what point did he postulate a common ancestor for ape and human?

He didn't in *The Origin of Species*, but in a later book.

What implications does this have theologically? After all, the Bible claims that we're made in the image of God.

Scientists seek to classify creatures on the basis of physical characteristics, and when we do that it is striking that humans very much resemble apes. That's where fossils found in Africa have played such a large part; they do seem to be filling the gap to a considerable degree. We find creatures that are clearly hominid – neither ape nor fully human; people put them into a sequence, and the exact sequence is a matter of debate. But that's the way the palaeontologist has to work, and it's based largely upon bone structure, cranial capacity, whether or not there is evidence of walking upright and so on.

And there is the use of tools.

Yes, though that goes beyond issues of structure and is more to do with evidence of cultural development.

The issue still is the biblical claim that humans are made in the image of God.

And how would we look for that? As far as the Bible is concerned, that is the key thing. It's a theological, a spiritual, definition. In the eighteenth and nineteenth centuries, when people thought about what makes us different from animals, they centred on two things. One was rationality, which can be related to a smooth sequence of developing brain capacity. But where do we put the dividing line between human and animal? The other difference is to do with morality. But we don't get evidence of morality until we have evidence for how people are living together. In terms of humans made in the image and likeness of God, the evidence we would look for is some evidence of belief in a supreme being and probably some kind of worship. As far as I know, the earliest evidence of worship is probably in a place in Turkey called Çatal Hüyük, where archaeologists think they have found rooms that were dedicated to worship activity going back to around 8000 BC, which is very, very recent. Others would say we get some sense of religion in cave paintings. I am not convinced by that. We may get some kind of evidence of a ritual to do with hunting, but no evidence of worship. Is burial evidence of belief in an afterlife, or just a sense of the importance of public hygiene? As we can see, it's very hard to make a dividing line. If we say that God used an evolutionary process to bring humans into being, this process is to do with physical structure. At what point, however, does this physical being have the ability to recognise and commune with God? We can relate the 'When?' question to the first evidence of worship, but as to how this happens, I don't think we will ever get an answer from science, because we have not yet solved the relationship between the mind and the brain. A sense of God, I think, must go with a sense of self-consciousness, a consciousness of ourselves and other beings. Without that, we can't be conscious of a supreme being. So all this is in some sense related to the developing complexity of our personality, which I suppose goes back to the complexity of the central nervous system. But at what point we could say we have a being in the image and likeness of God which has a sense of God in itself is something we won't ever answer scientifically.

Now, let's move on to looking at evolutionary theory in more detail. How does evolution 'work'?

To put it at its very simplest – first, there is the phenomenon of multiplication, the fact that most creatures have many offspring. The resources a creature lives on are limited. This leads to competition and the creatures that get the bigger share of the resources live longer, are healthier and have more offspring, to which they pass on their key characteristics.

Secondly, there is the observation of natural variety. Creatures differ from one another in size, strength, colour and so on. And it is these characteristics that make creatures more or less fit for the habitat, the environment in which they are competing for resources. This is called natural selection. So, for example, an animal that lives in woodland and is camouflaged is more likely to escape from predators, will live longer and is more likely to pass on that useful change in colour to the next generation.

That's the basic theory: natural variation; the competition for resources has a selective effect that triggers gradual change, which will eventually pass on to the whole population. Over time this gradual change in the nature of a species will become so great that we will have a different species.

One of the questions that arise is how this seemingly simple process could bring forth such complex organisms. Can we seriously believe that progress from an amoeba to Einstein is merely a question of natural selection and time?

Part of the answer to this is that the engine is not as simplistic as it seems. The more we know about genetics, the more we can see that the mechanism can become quite complex. We're not simply dealing with what are often called point mutations – one single change in one single gene. There is the possibility of much more complex things to happen within the genome.

The problem with the point mutation theory is that most mutations are neutral and that some are positively harmful.

True, but we now know that within the process of copying of genes sometimes a gene can be duplicated, so we end up with two copies of a particular gene. Now, when that happens, because the body only needs one working copy, the non-working copy of the gene can undergo mutation without affecting the viability of the organism. And there is evidence that once we have that second copy of a gene, mutations happen more rapidly. If the environment changes so that it makes the non-working, mutated copy of the gene more viable, that gene can kick in, so to speak. Take the rather complex blood-clotting system. This involves several similar protein molecules. There is reason to conclude that this system has arisen through the duplication of an original gene followed by mutations that have produced modified forms of the original protein that combine with it to produce a more effective clotting system.

Much more recently it was recognised that there are genes which control the way other genes work. If a mutation occurs there, we can end up with quite a major change happening in quite a short space of time, because a whole group of genes are linked to the control gene. Again, some of these changes in a control gene might be harmful. But we might get a change that is very positive.

Even so all of this seems to be happening within the boundaries of a species – micro-evolution. Still we aren't talking about macro-evolution – one species evolving into a new one.

This is a problem we have with any 'historical' theory. Evolution is a gradual, slow process; we'll never see it work in nature within the span of our lifetime. The argument will always have to be one of analogy. Take the human eye for example. Some species have a light sensitive patch on their skin. That's obviously of some survival value because it tells them when they're hidden from predators and when not. Then there are animals which have the light sensitive patch in a hollow. Once there's a hollow, there's a measure of directionality – where the light is coming from. When that hole is deepened we get a pinhole camera and images are formed. And if the hollow that gives the pinhole effect is filled with a kind of jelly, the eye becomes more efficient in terms of receiving an image. The pinhole covered with a membrane is the beginning of a lens. So we can look at these different types of eye, from the light sensitive patch to an eye with a stretchable lens, and can postulate a series of minor changes that will enable the process to go through. An interesting paper was published in the proceedings of the Royal Society, London, in 1994; a couple of biologists had calculated how many generations would be sufficient for a lens eye to evolve by natural selection, and they reckoned it would take 363,992 generations. That's about 7 million years, which is not very long.

What about the bigger scale changes, though, from one species to another – such as the path from amoeba to human being?

This kind of calculation, based on a modern understanding of genetics, does suggest that when we are talking billions of years, we have sufficient time for macro-evolution to take place. However mind-boggling the process is, there is the possibility of it happening.

Until the last few decades we were unable to do computer simulation games. There are now games which simulate the kind of
evolutionary changes that could happen, using a random process
– the mixture of random change and some kind of selection driving a process in the direction of increasing complexity.

But it is true, with a few exceptions, that all we ever observe in
the laboratory is micro-evolution, because we just haven't got the
time. Take the 363,992 generations of the development of the eye;
we are never going to observe that in a laboratory!

The exceptions are the result of the fact that in some organisms,
such as plants, there is sometimes a spontaneous doubling of the
number of chromosomes. This results in the formation of a new
species. An example of this is the appearance of *Spartina angelica*
in Southampton Water in the late nineteenth century.

*Popular science presents evolution as accepted fact. Are there more
debates among scientists going on behind the scenes than meets the
layperson's eye?*

There is very little debate among biologists about the principle
of evolution – variation leading to increasing complexity. The
overall framework is accepted. Where there is still considerable
debate it is about the details of the possible mechanisms. Some
prefer models of sudden evolutionary jumps, with changes in
the environment forcing natural selection to happen over several centuries – in other words, relatively rapidly. And there are
those who put much emphasis on gradual, slow change as it
was originally thought of by Darwin. So there is a heated internal debate about how evolution happens, but there is nonetheless a general assumption that evolution of some sort is the
answer to the variety of species that we see in the world today
and that they have originated from some single cell creature.
And there is much debate as to how the transition from an inorganic soup of chemicals to an organic single cell creature could
have happened.

It takes more than a few flashes of lightning for life to begin.

Absolutely!

Created?

When Darwin published his theory of evolution, there were those who managed to accommodate it into their Christian world-view. Others couldn't.

There's an interesting history here that people often aren't aware of. We need to go back to the beginning of the nineteenth century, when geology was the burgeoning science and people had begun to think of the world being much older than they had believed it to be. Go back even further to the seventeenth century and Archbishop Usher who, based on the genealogies of Genesis, calculated that the world was created in 4004 BC. I think he postulated 10 October for some reason and that figure got printed in Bibles. I remember as a child having a copy of the King James Bible which had 4004 BC written at the top of the page of Genesis 1. This fitted with the apocalyptic idea that the Earth is six thousand years old, and seven thousand years would be the Millennium. But by the 1800s, Christian scholars began to question this. As people looked at the many strata in the rocks, they became convinced that the Earth had a history. And they found that in the different strata there were different collections of fossils. This was well before Darwin and people simply used the fossils to identify particular strata. Initially this was for purely pragmatic reasons. Is this a water-bearing stratum, in which case one might want to make an Artesian well, or a water-holding stratum, in which case one could dig canals down and they wouldn't leak; or is it a stratum that is likely to bear certain metallic ores and is therefore worth mining? But people were struck by the fact that there were collections of fossils that seemed to be unique to particular strata – and, secondly, as strata were reached which were nearer the surface and therefore likely to be more recent, fossils became more complex. So people became aware that the Earth's history was much longer than 6,000 years.

What happened when Bible scholars were forced to take a fresh look at the Scriptures and the book of Genesis in particular?

One response was to treat the six days of creation as six epochs of any expandable length. A second idea was that Genesis might be only about the recent history of the Earth and that the creation described in Genesis chapter 1 is a recreation of the Earth. Finally, along came Darwin with his concept of millions of years.

Which wouldn't affect the two viewpoints you just described that much. But by the early twentieth century, a movement began to form in America that still exists today, which rejects evolution and promotes a young Earth.

There are several factors to consider here. On the social scale, there was a move from subsistent agriculture to the growth of the cities, the introduction of the assembly line and industrial-isation, all of which meant a growing divide between the city and the small town. The townspeople felt that the world was running away from them. But the changes were not just social but religious as well. The nineteenth century had seen the rise of biblical criticism and a seeming undermining of the author-ity of the Bible. It hit America later than Europe. In the 1920s, a series of pamphlets called *The Fundamentals* were published in the USA. Two of those pamphlets, which dealt with the subject of creation, weren't totally opposed to Darwinism but to athe-istic Darwinism that says that evolution is purely naturalistic; so they were in fact open to a process of evolution that God might have used. This reflects the Presbyterian background of *The Fundamentals*. The strong, Calvinistic, sense of God's sover-eignty leads the Calvinist theologian to say 'So what? God is sovereign and evolution might be the process that he chose to use.' The initial response in *The Fundamentals* pamphlets is that we can take on board, with some modification perhaps, the idea of evolution as long as God is in charge. But once it's athe-istic, we oppose it tooth and nail. However, what then hap-pened in the popular mind was that evolution as such came to be seen as an atheistic process. The initial opposition came not from mainstream Christianity but from Seventh Day Advent-ism. This goes back into the nineteenth century, with Ellen G. White, one of the founders of Seventh Day Adventism, who said that in the Ten Commandments it says that we should keep the Sabbath day holy. And the Sabbath day is the seventh day. Why are Christians worshipping on the first day of the week? Well, the orthodox Christian answer is that the first day is the day of the resurrection of Jesus, and in New Testament times we see a shift from worshipping on the seventh to the first day. But Ellen G. White said if we take the Bible literally we should worship on the Sabbath. She claimed that God had given her a revelation which said Genesis 1, where God rests on the seventh day after creating the world, had to be taken literally. So she understood the days of creation literally as seven twenty-four hour days.

In the early 1900s this was picked up by a Seventh Day Adventist, George McCready Price, who was a schoolteacher with some interest in geology. And he came up with the theory that all the fossils are a result of Noah's flood; a worldwide, catastrophic flood lays down the strata and all the fossils as the animals are buried under the water. His major publication was a book entitled *The New Geology*, published in 1923. That marks the beginning of so-called flood geology, which is used till today by short-term creationists to explain the evidence that Darwin had seen and interpreted as the history of natural selection and evolution.

So, short-term creationism started out as a fairly small movement. How did it come to such prominence in the USA today?

By the middle of the twentieth century, it was being picked up by Evangelicals in the United States in general. It may well be to do with continuing, rapid social change and the linking of Darwinism with all kinds of social evils. As modern genetics came to be understood, the eugenics movement started to grow, which says we can improve the human lot through genetics. In twentieth-century America, that became quite a popular – and, of course, a very racist – theory. It was then mixed up with Nazism, as Hitler took on eugenics in Europe; he defined those people whose life was not worth living – by which he meant the mentally or physically disabled and, of course, ultimately, the Jews. So Darwinism got a very bad press because of its association with the eugenics movement.

Didn't people see that Darwinism could also be used to argue for 'universal brotherhood', given that evolution proposed a common root for the human race?

Yes, we can draw an anti-racist message from Darwinism and, indeed, people have done this. But in the nineteenth century, people tended to categorise some races, particularly the 'negroes', as not truly human. So it all depends on how we read things. Of course the genetic evidence would be totally against the racist reading of Darwinism, but in the days of slavery and the lack of the knowledge of modern genetics, it was possible to read it a different way.

Back to short-term creationism. If someone believes in a literal, six-day, creation that took place some six thousand years ago, they have to read the Bible in a particular, i.e. literal, way.

What they will claim is that they are taking the Bible literally, which in a sense is a safer way of reading Scripture. There is a defensive kind of attitude here. Unless we can get certainty out of Scripture, we are imperilling our faith. And yet there are vast parts of Scripture that even the most diehard literalist does not take literally. Jesus says to pluck out one's eye if it causes one to sin and to cut off one's hand if it causes one to sin. I don't know anyone who takes that literally. Why? Because people recognise that we have to interpret. In this case we have to recognise figurative language – Jesus using hyperbole, exaggeration, to make a point; likewise, he uses figurative language in his parables.

Then there is a difference between poetry and prose. One of the weaknesses of the church's argument against Galileo was that it largely quoted biblical poetry – the Psalms – to back up its arguments. 'The LORD . . . has established the world; it shall never be moved' (Ps. 93:1, NRSV) is poetry but they were trying to read it as a basis for cosmology.

So people recognise that there are different types of text in the Scriptures, and yet some insist that Genesis 1 must be read literally, or else we're not taking it seriously; whereas other Christians would say we take it seriously by asking, 'What sort of literature is it?'

And what's your answer, as an Old Testament scholar?

One way to answer the question 'What sort of literature is Genesis?' is to look at other sorts of literature that were around at the time when it was written. So we're talking about the Ancient Near East somewhere between 1500 and 500 BC. In those days, society wasn't changing as rapidly as it is today, so we don't get much change in literature during that period. And we find that, at the time, there were other creation stories around from Egypt and Mesopotamia; we also have some Canaanite stories about Baal, so we can see how people wrote about the origins of the world and the human race in that cultural setting. At the heart of the Christian faith is the idea of incarnation, that God made himself known in a particular human being, in a particular culture at a particular time, speaking a particular language – and that is how God has always made himself known in the Judeo-Christian tradition. So we would expect that whoever wrote Genesis was inspired by God to write it in the terms of their culture and the literary forms of their day. That's where we find people writing about creation through, some would say, myth, some would say figurative and symbolic, rather than literal, language.

When we use the word 'myth' nowadays, we usually mean something like fairy tales. This is not how we understand myth in this context, is it?

The popular definition of 'myth' is something that is not true. But the technical use of the term by biblical scholars is seeking to explain the significance of the origin of things in a story which is not to be taken literally. The truth is embedded in the story.

Another way of looking at this is to analyse the text itself. What clues are there within the text as to how we are meant to read it? It's very interesting to go back to early Christian Bible commentators who aren't in any way embroiled in modern debates about science. Origen[9] says he reads Genesis 1 and he finds that sun, moon and stars aren't created until day four, but there are mornings and evenings on days one, two and three. Clearly, this is not to be taken literally; this is some kind of figurative narrative and Origen concludes that no sensible person would read it any other way. What the text is really saying is that the world is a planned, structured and ordered universe, and this is put across in a figurative account that has the semblance of history. Creation appears to be a week's work, but that is only a figure of speech to express that this is an ordered world. The first three days are about things being shaped, the next three days are about the shapes being filled with content. Nearer our time, Jean Calvin makes another important point. He is a good enough biblical scholar to have learnt Hebrew, and as he gets to the firmament mentioned in Genesis 1:8 he recognises that the Hebrew word for firmament implies a piece of beaten metal. He concludes that if we want to learn about astronomy we need to go elsewhere; don't go to Genesis 1, which is describing the world as people see it. To us the sky looks like a dome. We have the phrase in the Old Testament that the heavens look like brass (Deut. 28:23) and in the Middle East the summer sky sometimes does look like a copper bowl overhead. All Genesis 1 is saying is that the sky was made by God and not that the sky is made out of metal. This is a figure of speech, the language of appearance, as Calvin puts it. He applies the same to the sun and moon, which are referred to as the two great lights, whereas in Calvin's day astronomers had already concluded that Saturn was bigger than the moon. So again the Bible is using the language of appearance.

Calvin was predisposed to read the text as seven days, but for him the important point was that this is a piece of teaching presented in a way that will enable common people to understand the essence and meaning of creation.

You said that in the Ancient Near East there were competing creation myths. What is unique about Genesis?

The biggest difference is that in Genesis there is only one God. In the other texts there are not only many gods, but we also find the idea of an opposing force, usually depicted as waters of chaos. The Babylonian story adds monsters in the waters of chaos, which are defeated by the creator god in battle. In Genesis 1, there is no battle for creation; God just speaks and things happen. Mesopotamian religion was anxiety-ridden. There was always the fear that the forces of chaos had been overcome only temporarily. They were locked out of the universe but they were still there. None of that in Genesis 1, because there were no forces of chaos to start with! The structure created by the God of Genesis is stable for good.

What about the place of human beings in creation?

They are the pinnacle of creation in Genesis 1. That is indicated in two ways. God deliberates before he creates them: 'Let us make man in our image' (Gen. 1:26, NIV). Then it is said three times – another piece of poetry there – that God created humans in his image (Gen. 1:27); so humans have a very special place as his representatives in creation. A lot of ink has been spilt over the question of what it means to be made in the image of God. I think the simplest way to understand it is that we represent God on Earth, that we must be of such a nature that we can reflect something of God in our human personality. This is what makes Incarnation possible, the message of the New Testament that God can become a human being.

Whereas in the other creation myths, humans appear to be more like the playthings of the gods.

Yes. Once Marduk has created the world in the Babylonian story, some of the gods who sided with the forces of chaos are punished and have to live on the earth and grow the food and build the houses for the other gods. Here we are into the idea of the temple, sacrifices and so on. They get fed up with doing this, because they are, after all, gods. This is the first recorded strike. They refuse to do the work, whereupon Marduk has the great idea that he will make human beings to take over. That's the sole purpose of human beings in Babylonian mythology: to build houses for the gods and to provide them with food and drink. By the way, in social terms, being slaves of the gods ends up as being slaves of the temple and, as the temple is part of the city-state, this means being slaves of the city-state.

Another striking element of Genesis 1 is that sun and moon are not divine beings.

That's right; having many gods almost always ends up in them being personifications of natural forces or natural entities like the sun and the moon. In Babylonian religion, Marduk is the sun god. But in Genesis 1, sun and moon are just lights, calendar markers, there to serve humans and not vice versa.

So, going back to a literalist approach to Genesis 1, is the literalist reader, frankly, missing the point?

They are trying to read the text as if it should be excavated for scientific information. The danger of that is that we miss the theological message.

Moving on to the New Testament – didn't the New Testament writers repeatedly refer to Genesis 1 and indeed, it seems, take the account literally?

That's because God's revelation comes to us in an incarnated form. It comes in the form of the original writers, who wrote for their specific culture. That said, a number of New Testament scholars have argued that, say, when Paul talks about Adam, he is really thinking of Adam as an archetype, as a representative figure from which he draws a theological lesson, rather than an individual, historical being.

Calvin asked the question, 'Who was Cain's wife?' and pointed out that when God drives Cain out of Eden, Cain expresses fear that whoever finds him will kill him. So, Calvin says, the implication is, there were other human beings around at the time, and that God chose Adam and Eve as a representative couple who were faced with the challenge, will they obey their creator or not? So, it's not the genetic relationship that is important but it's the representative role of Adam and Eve.

In terms of evolution, one could argue that when Homo sapiens get to the point where they have self-consciousness and consciousness of God, they are inevitably faced with the question of whether to obey God or go their own way.

It is not the purpose of our conversation, and indeed this book, to elaborate on the creationist critique of evolution from a scientific point of

view. But I do want to mention at least one of the chief areas of criticism:
the problem of time. If the Earth is not billions of years old, but young,
the whole system of slow, gradual evolutionary change collapses. How
reliable, then, is the radio-metric dating of rocks and fossils, really?

Short-term creationists tend to recycle examples which go back to
the early days of using radio-metric dating some decades ago.
One example I've seen repeated several times in creationist literature is the dating of lava which radio-metric dating suggested
was very old, when people knew that the lava had only been
produced a couple of hundred or so years ago. What the experi-
menters realised was that as the lava had come up through the
volcanic vents, it had broken off bits of rock which were much
older, and when they crushed the lava they also crushed some
tiny bits of old rock, which is what they measured. When they
had made sure that they had only got crushed lava, they got the
right sort of date. Examples like that are recycled without
explaining why there was originally an error.

Another problem is in the early use of Carbon 14 dating, that
is, measuring radioactive decay. In the early days it wasn't fully
understood how C14 is produced in the atmosphere by the
impacts of cosmic radiation and how that had caused considerable fluctuations in the concentration of C14 – and that therefore
its use for dating was not straightforward. So initially, scientists
sometimes got some very strange results. But nowadays we can
work round that. It's a question of methodology, not the principle.

What about the assumption that radioactive decay continues at a con-
stant rate over billions of years?

Our understanding of why radioactive elements are radioactive
and break down is based on subatomic quantum theory. On the
basis of that theory we can understand why the breakdown rate
is constant and not affected by things like the amount of cosmic
radiation, temperature or whatever. Different radioactive elements are used for dating, and as we use the different elements
we get a similar result, which suggests the dating may be reliable.
Secondly, there is something called the Isochron method, which

validates the assumption of a constant rate of decay. Thirdly, by dating the age of stars in star clusters, we can date the age of galaxies; that's a completely different methodology which depends on our understanding of nuclear fusion. We end up with an age of the galaxies of some 10 billion years, while radio-metric dating dates the Earth at about 4.5 billion. The figures are all in the same ballpark, which suggests that these methodologies are reliable.

Designed?

In the debate on the origin and development of life, evolution and short-term creationism were joined recently by a new idea: Intelligent Design. What are the main points?

Intelligent Design takes us back to David Hume's response to the design argument. How do we know when something in nature is designed, as opposed to having come about purely by natural laws and forces? The strength of Dembski's[10] approach, for example in his book *The Design Inference*,[11] is that he has tried to put figures on the design argument. He comes at it as a statistician, asking how we can estimate the probability of a complex system coming into being by chance. He seeks to set up a minimal threshold of probability beyond which it becomes very improbable for a particular system to come into being. The problem is, in some of his more popular writings he seems to shift from saying 'This is improbable' to saying 'This is impossible'; in other words, he claims that he has proved something to be impossible when all that he has shown is that it is improbable. There are also problems in the ways in which he calculates the probabilities.

How does this relate to the Intelligent Design concept of 'irreducible complexity'?

This is connected with Michael Behe,[12] a biochemist who argues that when we have a very complex biological system, it becomes impossible to envisage how that system could have come into being by a process of gradual change, because the system would only work and be of survival value as a complete system. Remove one element from the mechanism and it stops being a workable system and is therefore no longer of any survival value. This is what he means by an 'irreducibly complex' system; it can't be reduced any further to simple components that would have evolved independently and then come together to give us the complex mechanism.

One famous, some would say infamous, example is the bacterial flagellum.

Indeed, some bacteria have a whip-like appendage called the flagellum (from Latin: whip). The bacteria use the flagellum for propulsion; so they can move forwards and backwards in whatever fluid they are in. The analogy Behe uses is that of a boat with an outboard motor. An outboard motor is of no use unless you have a unit of three components working together – motor, propeller, and rudder. Each on their own are of little value. The same, says Behe, holds for the bacteria. They have, as it were, an inbuilt 'motor' that provides the power to rotate the flagellum; they also have a 'propeller shaft' that links the 'motor' with the flagellum; and, finally, the flagellum acts like a propeller and a rudder to direct the bacterium. All of these together are needed to enable the bacterium to move.

That seems to make sense.

Yes, except people have pointed out that it's not that simple, because there are bacteria which have just a flagellum – and that is of value to them. It can be used both to capture food and for bacteria to link themselves together, which is of survival value for the bacteria in certain situations. So the flagellum on its own does have some survival value. Then, there are bacteria that only have the 'propeller shaft' but that is also useful on its own as it is hollow and is used for excretion of waste chemicals. Finally, we get bacteria which have the shaft and the motor that rotates the shaft; and the value of that seems to be that when a fluid is pumped out of a rotating shaft, the waste is pushed further away than if it were simply pumped out. So each of the three – the shaft, the propeller and the motor – can be of survival value without them being combined in a system. Therefore we can postulate the possibility that the three parts did exist separately before they came together. In support of this, even where the flagellum is used for movement, it is still hollow and is being used for chemical waste disposal.

Nonetheless, the whole mechanism, all the information that controls the bacterium, is so intricate that it seems hard to believe that all this could have simply developed by blind chance.

The question you're asking is, 'If we start with chance, how do we end up with order?' But we do know that this does happen. In simple chemical systems we can get order out of what seems to be chaos, provided we are pumping in energy. For example, there are chemical systems which will change from one colour to another and back again as regular as clockwork as long as energy is pumped into them to keep the reaction going and stop them reaching a state of chemical equilibrium. Such systems are called 'self-ordering systems'. This is related to the second law of thermodynamics. Normally we move from a system of order to a system of disorder, but we can buck the system by putting in energy, which enables us to establish order in one small area but at the expense of disorder in other areas. The growing of leaves on trees in spring for instance, is a highly ordered process. The ordered structure of the leaf comes from the energy of the sunlight. The pay-off is we're getting increasing disorder in the sun. As the sun burns up its fuel, producing the heat and light that allows for life on Earth, it is becoming chemically and physically more disordered while Earth is becoming more ordered. So we can get order out of disorder via energy transmission.

Now, in terms of natural selection, there is indeed chance in mutation but we have an ordering grid, namely the pressures of the habitat that govern natural selection, which imposes order on chance mutations. This is where computer simulation programs come in to show that this can happen. In industry nowadays they use random search programs in order to carry out certain forms of planning. To use an example, one of the most efficient ways of designing aircraft wings is to use random search programs. We enter our constraints into the program but don't set it out in a logical, step-by-step process; the program puts in random changes, which turns out to be the quickest way to get the right design out at the other end. So we can imagine evolution as a random search program that God uses to create life on Earth and produce humans, whereby the constraints God puts in are the nature of matter and the laws of nature.

I have come across a critique of Intelligent Design as not being proper science; rather than investigating systems, people just shrug their shoulders and say it's irreducibly complex.

That's slightly unfair. But there is the danger of concluding too readily that something is irreducibly complex and therefore we give up trying to explain how a system could have come into being. But at least in theory the Intelligent Design approach is open to testing.

As for Dembski, I'm not sure we are in a position to do the calculations he does on probability, because our knowledge of biological systems is so limited at the moment. Back in the 1960s, I was working on enzymes, which are proteins. Think of proteins as a bead necklace. Think of the sub-units – amino acids – as the beads and the protein as a string of beads. At that time, people calculated the probability of a protein coming into being by chance. Let's say a small protein may be made up of 200 beads. We know there are about twenty different kinds of amino acids ('beads') in naturally occurring proteins. It was assumed that it was important to have each bead in the right place. The probability of the first bead being in the right place is 1:20, for the second bead it's 1:20 x 20, and so we keep multiplying. If we have a protein that is 200 beads long, the probability of getting there is 1 divided by 20 x 20 x 20 . . . 200 times. Multiplying twenty by itself 200 times is a big number. By what we knew about proteins at the time, that seemed a reasonable calculation. However, once we knew more about protein structure through crystallising them, using X-rays to look at the structure, it became apparent that there are two basic types of amino acids. There are 'water-loving' (water soluble) ones and 'water-hating' (not very soluble in water) ones. The water-soluble amino acids gathered on the outside of a globular, ball-like protein and the water hating ones on the inside. So perhaps the calculation should not be probability 1:20 but 1:2. Is the amino acid water-loving or water-hating? Thereby we end up with a much smaller number because we are not multiplying twenty by itself 200 times, but two. That's simplistic because the process is more complex in reality, but it does show that the calculation might be many orders of magnitude out if we don't understand the structure of the protein. I suspect the same might be true about the bacterial flagellum or the blood-clotting system; we just don't know enough about them to do a credible calculation that will back up the claim that they are irreducibly complex. Once we do know enough, we may find that the figure of improbability is a lot smaller than Dembski says it is.

Intelligent Design has been accused by some Christians of promoting the old God of the gaps. Earlier, you mentioned Isaac Newton finding 'irreducible complexities' in the solar system,[13] which were resolved later without resorting to God. Do you agree that Intelligent Design is prone to fall into the same trap?

I think it is Intelligent Design's main philosophical weakness. They will protest that they are not talking about the God of the gaps, because they say, 'We can do the calculations! It's not a matter of showing our ignorance; we are showing that it's impossible.' If we accept that, Intelligent Design may not be presenting a God of the gaps but a God who is an incompetent creator. This was Leibniz' response to Newton: the implication being that God was not up to creating a stable universe. And that's my major objection to Intelligent Design; it implies that God is not capable of designing a seamless process which could produce a complex system. Most proponents of Intelligent Design are willing to accept evolution beyond the single species. But there are certain points where, if you like, the problem gets too big for God and he has to step in and tinker with the system to produce a particular, irreducibly complex, bit before there can be any further development. That may be unfair, but that's what it seems to be. For me the biblical view of God is of One who is wise and powerful enough to bring into being a universe that is seamless.

Darwin, Man and God

Atheists like Richard Dawkins will tell you that there is no more evidence for God than the tooth fairy and that Darwinism does not suggest but indeed compels us to atheism.

I can see why he is saying that agnosticism or atheism might seem more of an option after Darwin than before. There is a psychological factor here; the fact that Christians have invested so much in the design argument, which Darwinism seemed to destroy. So we can conclude that if there is no evidence for a designer then perhaps there is no designer. But this option is certainly not compelling. As we said earlier, many nineteenth century Christians had no problem accepting Darwinism. I mentioned Christians from the Reformed tradition for example, who had a strong sense of God's sovereignty over the process of history; so why shouldn't he have sovereignty over the processes of nature? But this is equally true of people of other Christian traditions. Anglicans like Charles Kingsley or Archbishop Frederick Temple found it possible to incorporate Darwinism. In fact, what both of them say in their writings is that Darwin has given them a more inspiring concept of God; a God who could design and oversee this kind of process seemed even more awe-inspiring than one who created numerous individual creatures at one point in time. There is something of that even in Richard Dawkins as he talks about the awesomeness of nature and the process of evolution. But he stops there. He doesn't go on to ask whether it is more reasonable to think of it all as a pure chance process or whether there might be something more to be said about it.

You mentioned Calvinists and Anglicans; one prominent Catholic was Pierre Teilhard de Chardin.[14]

Perhaps he was the first person to develop systematically a macro-evolutionary theology, though I do think it has its problems. I don't quite see how he correlates what he calls the 'cosmic Christ' – what he sees as the goal of the process and what he calls the Omega Point – with the incarnate Christ, who becomes incarnate within the evolutionary process. Other people have commented that there is an unsatisfactory attempt to deal with the issue of original sin. But at any rate, Teilhard didn't see Darwinism to be in conflict with Christian theology.

One core question raised by Intelligent Design was how information and complexity could arise from chance. How would theistic evolution answer that?

We have information in the nature of matter and the laws of the universe. God has given the information, which is transferred into various forms. So it's not information appearing out of nowhere. It's a question that is harder to answer for the atheistic evolutionist, because they have to postulate that information comes out of chaos.

If we conclude from what we've seen so far that evolution is the best model we have at present to explain the variety of life on our planet, we are left, on a philosophical level, with two options: theistic and atheistic evolution. Either life on Earth has evolved without any divine interven- tion, or God is steering the process. One problem with the latter is to conceive of a benevolent God creating a system that relies on ruthless competition, the survival of the fittest and an incredible amount of wastage of life.

There's no simple answer but there are a number of considera- tions. The traditional Christian reply to the problem of evil is that human beings have received a measure of free will. We can expect God to do miracles but not to do something that is logi- cal nonsense. And to create a robot that freely chooses to love you is nonsense. That is what the story in Genesis chapter 3 is partly about. Adam and Eve are given the challenge to obey their creator and they choose to disobey. That's where evil and suffering enters into the world. Now it seems to me that, in the Bible, death is an evil for human beings; Paul says 'the sting of death is sin' (1 Cor. 15:56, NRSV). But it can't be an evil in the same way for beings that aren't self-conscious and have no con- scious relationship with God. So the physical death of non- human creatures needn't be seen as an evil in itself, but just a fact of life.

As for pain, the question is whether pain and suffering are the same. We have self-consciousness; we can face the question: 'Why should I suffer?' We have memory of painful experiences that may affect us for a long time. But for creatures that lack self-consciousness, is pain an evil? Pain is a reaction, which sometimes has very positive uses; it can get us out of a dangerous situation. With regard to wastage – why some 90 per cent of all the species that have ever lived died out – again, it is wastage when we look at it from a purely human point of view.

Part of our creativity is that we can enjoy the process of creating even without regard to the end product, though of course a good end product makes it even more satisfying. If that is something that reflects the nature of God, then it doesn't surprise me that God should use a process that involves extinct species that were enjoyed by God while they were alive. So from God's point of view, they would not have been wasted.

How, then, are we to understand the repeated statements in Genesis chapter 1, that God saw that what he had created was 'good'?

The Hebrew word that is used here, *tob*, has a wide range of meanings. In fact it is only fairly rarely used in the sense 'morally good'. It often means 'aesthetically pleasing', and 'beautiful'. That could be the meaning here. However, a common meaning of it that makes sense here is 'fit for purpose'. The way the account is written indicates that part of the purpose is that it should be an environment in which human beings can live and develop as creatures who are responsible moral beings and answerable to their creator.

And, of course, the theory of evolution was not the first to raise the theodicy problem – how can God be good and omnipotent in the face of evil and suffering; that question riddled people long before Darwin.

Yes; evolution perhaps increases the problem in size, but it's the same issue in principle.

In Christianity the problem of evil is intimately linked with Genesis chapter 3 – the story of Adam and Eve eating from the tree of the knowledge of good and evil in spite of God's command – and interpreted solely in terms of disobedience, of the original sin that affects all of humanity from that day forward. But the account also seems to talk about Adam and Eve growing up from animal-like, ethical ignorance; a decisive step in the evolution of Homo sapiens, if you will.

Yes, we can read the story in terms of growth of understanding, as they eat from the tree of knowledge. Irenaeus[15] pointed out the fact that, prior to the Fall, Adam and Eve are like children. It's important to recognise that the picture we're given is that they are innocent, not that they are perfect. Often we think of Eden as perfection, but the Bible talks of innocence which Adam and Eve lose in return for knowledge of good and evil, and they then have a sense of shame and guilt. And yes, that can be seen in terms of moral growth. But what the passage is saying is that there are two pathways of growth: they could develop through continuing dependence on God, or through disobedience, which, however, leads to the need for salvation in the Christian understanding.

If we accept both evolution and Christianity, we will conclude that humanity is the pinnacle of a God-driven evolutionary process. Darwinism, of course, predicts that over time species will continue to evolve into ever more complex ones. In other words, it appears that Homo sapiens would not be the be-all and end-all of the created world.

The key moment in Christian chronology is the Incarnation – God becoming man in Jesus, which makes possible forgiveness and a personal relationship with God that will continue for eternity. If in God's purposes the Earth continues for millions of years, it is likely that humans will evolve into some other sort of being, though in terms of the Darwinian physical theory the principle of the survival of the fittest no longer applies to human beings, as we now make our own environment. So, if you like, we choose our own evolution by the social and environmental changes we make. But whatever type of human being there may be far in the future, the Christian would still point to the possibility of a relationship with God, whatever type of human being we're talking about.

The concept of biological evolution is based on survival advantage in a competitive natural environment. What of those human characteristics that appear to have no survival value in themselves, such as music, art, or indeed higher mathematics, which goes beyond the pragmatic usefulness of arithmetic but touches on metaphysics and the mystery of the universe?

That reminds me of a Sherlock Holmes story. Holmes is looking at a rose and commenting on its beauty. He says that beauty is not a necessity but an extra and that the fact that we can appreciate beauty, for him, is evidence for the existence of God. I think there is some validity to that. To a certain level, aesthetics does have some survival value. Many creatures, for instance, exist without colour vision, but colour vision can be helpful to warn against certain dangerous plants, for example. As for music, birds use it as warning signs or mating calls, but the complexity of music we can create and enjoy goes beyond anything necessary for survival. Likewise, the language of poetry goes beyond the essential need for communication. Indeed, to me this is more readily understandable in terms of humans being made in the image of God than as the result of the pure chance process postulated by the atheist evolutionist.

Equivalent Models?

We've been looking at three models to account for the source and variety of life – creationism, Intelligent Design and evolution. Can you sum up the strengths and weaknesses of each model?

I find it very difficult to find any strength in short-term creationism, except that I do appreciate the motivation of wanting to take the Bible seriously and to be faithful to it. I think the weakness is that those who hold the position assume that to be faithful to the Bible always means taking it literally, whereas it seems to me that it's about taking the Bible seriously. To take it seriously we need to ask the question, 'What kind of literature am I reading? What kind of language is being used here?' To fail to do that leads to misunderstanding and misinterpretation. If we take what is meant to be figurative language as literal language, it can lead us into quite serious error.

Another weakness is that short-term creationists have to spend so much energy trying to – from my point of view – explain away the scientific evidence for evolution. It's very negative; they are constantly trying to dig holes rather than contributing something positive to the understanding of the world.

And short-term creationism seems to be giving Christianity an anti-intellectual image.

Short-term creationists will say that they are seeking to be as intellectual as other scientists by trying to prove them wrong on their own grounds, but what comes across is a closed-minded, defensive attitude that leads to torturous arguments which don't convince the outsider. Unfortunately, for many people this becomes a turn-off not just for short-term creationism but the Bible as such.

Your take on teaching creationism in schools?

I don't think it should be taught. Of course it should get a mention in religious education as a way of understanding the world, but it should not be taught as something that is on a level with evolutionist scientific theories.

What about the pros and cons of Intelligent Design?

One of its pros is that, consciously or not, it is seeking to respond to David Hume's critique of the design argument; how we decide whether something was designed by a conscious agent or whether it came about by a natural process. Intelligent Design takes this criticism seriously; it tries to quantify and identify systems of which we can say that they are probably designed.

The problem with Intelligent Design is that, once we admit the probability of Intelligent Design, we remove some of the motivation for doing science, for continuing to study a complex system. As for its methodology, I don't think we have the knowledge or capability for quantifying accurately, as I illustrated earlier through the attempt to estimate the probability of a protein coming into being by chance. That chance initially seemed incredibly small. But as we got to know more about the structure of the protein, we realised that the probability was far higher. So we don't yet have the knowledge of the individual steps leading to a complex system to do Dembski's probability calculations in a reliable and accurate way. Ultimately, there is a theological problem with Intelligent Design. It gives the picture of a God who either hasn't got the wisdom or the power to produce a seamless process.

So we're back at the God of the gaps. There are things we can't explain, so somehow God must have stepped in to make them work.

Indeed; though proponents of Intelligent Design would argue that we can quantify probabilities; so this is not about gaps of ignorance but the real impossibility of something coming about by chance. But I would say that the 'impossibilities' really do come down to a gap of ignorance.

Finally, in a nutshell, what are the strengths and weaknesses of the evolutionary model?

There is a big gap in understanding the development from inorganic chemicals to the first living cell. There are a few possibilities. One is to do with RNA, a molecule which acts as a messenger in many living cells, taking the DNA information from the nucleus out into the cell where the information enables the right proteins to be produced. People have found cases where RNA is self-replicating, and this might indicate that the first living organisms did not operate on DNA as the information storage and RNA as the information messenger, but RNA itself as both the store and the messenger. DNA would have replaced it eventually, because it is a more stable molecule and therefore a more suitable information store. But even so, the question still remains where the RNA came from.

Another possibility is that some clays have a catalytic effect on certain chemical reactions that might be of biological importance. So those may have been the stepping stones from inorganic matter to living cells. But this may just be straws in the wind and there is a big hole in our understanding.

Another weakness is that we have very few examples of one species transforming into another, especially in the more complex organisms.

But then that is in the nature of the theory – gradual processes taking a long time; something we will never be able to replicate in the laboratory.

On the other hand, the main strength of evolutionary theory is that it enables us to make sense of what otherwise would be a lot of disparate facts, and that it allows us to make predictions. Some of these can, and have been, tested by observation, especially at the level of molecular biology.

Scientists tend to make the assumption that scientific answers are the complete, or at any rate the only reliable, answers. But, inevitably, once they try to touch on the Why questions, they start to bring in something from outside science. One of the classic cases is Jacques Monod's[16] book *Chance and Necessity*,[17] in which he claims that science supports existentialist philosophy, that we live in a soulless, mindless universe in which we are just products of chance. And he ends his book by saying that what gives life meaning is to face up to this fact. How that would give us meaning I don't know. But at least he's upfront about the fact that his philosophy is informing his interpretation of scientific findings. With writers like Dawkins or Atkins[18] it is less clear that they are conscious of bringing a world-view to their interpretation of science.

Therefore, it is equally justified to interpret our science within a theistic framework. In my view, evolution paints an awesome picture of God. It doesn't shut God out of the naturalistic process, because the natural laws are not to be understood as some impersonal processes but as God's faithful activity in sustaining his world. I think it is going too far to say that science proves the Christian world-view. But it is valid to keep saying to people that they are not in conflict with one another.

3.

The Faith

In the previous two chapters, Ernest Lucas attempted to show that neither cosmology nor biology is fit to prove or disprove God. Not only do theological questions lie outside the realm of science, but even if we do decide to link scientific findings with philosophical reflection, we can use them to argue either for or against God's existence. Christianity, however, goes a decisive step farther. We are no longer talking about the possible existence of some cosmic spirit, some universal intelligence, but about a transcendent, supreme being revealed in the 'God-man', Jesus Christ. This leads us to the final question in our conversation on faith and science. It is the one we asked at the outset – whether Christianity's impact on Western culture and spirituality is diminishing because its core concepts are incompatible with our twenty-first century knowledge of the world.

As we have seen, believers in Christ have been exposed to an increasing amount of rationalist gunfire since the days of the Enlightenment; Darwinism, at least on a popular level, continued to fuel the scepticism and widen the gap between science and religion. By the twentieth century, the established Christian world-view was pulled into question once again – this time, however, from within its own ranks.

Few of the tourists strolling along the picturesque streets of Marburg may be aware that the quiet German university town was, at one point, the hub of another 'Copernican' revolution, this time in biblical scholarship. Some nineteenth-century theologians had already started to shake heavily Christianity's old foundations by redefining its teachings in the context of a changing intellectual and spiritual climate. By the 1920s, however, biblical criticism within the Christian camp reached new heights. Rudolf Bultmann (1884–1976), New Testament professor at Marburg University, was setting out to 'demythologise' the Scriptures, to show that the pre-scientific world-view of the biblical authors, and the four Evangelists in particular, precluded any face-value interpretation of their writings. The story of Jesus was essentially a mesh of myth and legend, with a few loose ends of actual history. Traditional Christian orthodoxy had turned into a type of existentialist philosophy with little factual underpinning. So, once more, we are led to look at faith – the gospel of Christ – on the one hand, and science – the findings of biblical scholarship – on the other.

Gospel Truth

Dr Lucas, in what way did Bultmann pose what can be called an unparalleled challenge to traditional Christian interpretations of the Scriptures?

Bultmann reflects the dominance of Enlightenment rationalism, which affected a whole range of academic disciplines and came into biblical studies via its effect upon historical studies. It's to do with the concept of writing scientific history; in other words, a recording of history that was based on principles and evidence, rather than anecdotes. One of these was the principle of analogy; we think about the past in terms of an analogy of what we experience today. Once we do that, we obviously run into problems with things like miracles. Scholars like Bultmann would be very sceptical of any writing of history which includes God as an actor and events that are attributed to God rather than human beings. That became an issue for biblical scholars. As a New Testament scholar, Bultmann was concerned with the Gospels, where we find many miracles. And that posed a problem.

At the same time, Europe saw the growth of existentialist philosophy with its emphasis on the importance of the experience of the individual – in Germany, Martin Heidegger[1] in particular – and that flowed into Bultmann's methodology. So Bultmann is happy to talk, say, about the resurrection of Jesus in terms of the disciples having an experience of the risen Christ which was real for them. But we don't have to tie this down to a physical body disappearing from a tomb as an act of God. That's not really the important thing, Bultmann would say; it's the disciples' experience that counts.

Two things are coming together here; the Enlightenment scepticism about God acting in history, and existentialist philosophy that says the most important thing is the individual's experience.

The trend of reading the Bible as a document of human religious experience, over and above the Bible as the Word of God, had started a century earlier, with thinkers like Friedrich Schleiermacher.² On the other hand, the nineteenth century saw a growing interest in reconstructing the life of Jesus.

This ties in with the new understanding of history. We get New Testament scholars who want to be historians, and therefore try to apply the new historical methodology to the Gospels to write an account of the historical Jesus. So, on the one hand there is a stress upon the rich experience of Jesus; on the other hand, scholars are trying to produce an objective account of the historical Jesus. This leads to a growing divergence of scholars talking about the Christ of faith and the Jesus of history and debating the connection between the two, and which is the more important.

Bultmann claimed that we could know very little about the Jesus of history because we don't know whether the Gospels are historically accurate, but he also said that it didn't matter. What mattered was the religious experience, the existential dimension. This take seems to be the dominant one today.

Well, I do think there has been a reaction against Bultmann in academic circles. The 1960s and seventies saw a new quest for the historical Jesus. The reaction implied that we couldn't write the sort of scientific history that in the late nineteenth and early twentieth centuries some liberal scholars had been seeking to produce, and some conservatives had claimed they could write. But we could produce a portrait, if you like, rather than a photograph. That approach has gone a fair way, saying that we can affirm that there was a historical Jesus and we can say certain things about him.

What's the lowest common denominator?

It is three-fold. First of all, we can look for evidence outside the New Testament – and there is some. Not surprisingly, not a vast amount, because in his own day Jesus was not a very important person, but an artisan in a backwater of the Roman Empire. Nonetheless, there are writers in the first and second centuries who mention him. There is Thallus, probably a Samaritan writer; Josephus, the Jewish historian, and some of the Roman historians – Tacitus, Pliny and Suetonius. If we put together what they say we get the picture of a Jewish teacher who was known as a miracle-worker, who gathered followers around him, was condemned to crucifixion by Pilate, the Roman procurator of Judea in the time of Tiberius, and that some time after his death his followers were claiming that he was alive again. That's the sort of minimal picture we can draw from outside the New Testament. So no one would doubt that Jesus was a real person who lived in the first part of the first century and whose impact went beyond his crucifixion.

Secondly, what can we say about Jesus, looking at the New Testament? Scholars point out that it's quite striking that a good deal of the sayings of Jesus, while they were written down in Greek, can be translated back into good Aramaic. And we would expect Jesus to have taught in Aramaic because that was the language of the common people in his day. Scholars will debate which of the recorded sayings can be attributed to Jesus and which cannot, but they certainly accept that he was a Jewish teacher who taught about the kingdom of God, who talked about God breaking into the world to save his people, and who claimed to have a central place within this work of God, which was the fulfilment of the Old Testament promise of God bringing about a new covenant. As for the accounts of what Jesus did in detail, there may be more debate among scholars, but few would deny that he had a reputation as an exorcist casting out demons. The debate is whether to interpret these as psychosomatic healings, but it is accepted that he had a reputation as a healer, whatever happened in detail. There is a wide consensus among modern-day scholars on this picture of Jesus.

Thirdly, it is generally accepted that he had a lasting influence and that, within a few decades of his death, there were people claiming that he was God. If we go back to the early part of the twentieth century, people claimed that Jesus' followers made him into God after his death once the church had become increasingly Gentile, as the pagans were used to deifying and worshipping great heroes after they had died. But again, increasingly scholars have reacted against this, because the evidence we have in the Gospels is that this deifying of Jesus goes back to the earliest generation of the Christian church, when it was still mainly Jewish and Aramaic-speaking. This is because some of the confessions in the New Testament reflect Aramaic, for instance the prayer *'Maranatha!'* which is used by Paul and in the book of Revelation and is an Aramaic word for 'Our Lord come!'. The striking thing about this is the use of the word *'Mara'* – Lord – of Jesus, because we now know that in Qumran and elsewhere that was the term used by Jews in Aramaic to refer to the God of the Old Testament, the equivalent of the Hebrew Adonai – my Lord. Now, if we find Aramaic Christians using that terminology of Jesus, it must go back to the very early years of the church. Outside of the New Testament *'Maranatha!'* is used in another early Christian writing, the *'Didache'*, in the context of the Eucharist. It is written in Greek but uses the Aramaic term. So it seems to have become part of the Christian faith very early on.

Then there are phrases in Paul's letters. In 1 Corinthians 8, Paul is talking about a very practical, mundane issue; should Christians eat food that has been offered to pagan idols? Paul says that the idols aren't real gods because there is only one God and one Lord through whom we exist. According to most scholars, Paul is echoing the Jewish confession that there is one God and one Lord, which is called the Shema and goes back to the book of Deuteronomy. Today, the orthodox Jew prays this prayer every day. The thing to grasp is that Paul seems to change 'one God and Lord' into 'one God, the Father . . . and one Lord, Jesus Christ' (v.6, NRSV). For Paul, who came from a Jewish background, this was an amazing thing to do.

Then there's that wonderful piece of poetry in Paul's letter to the Philippians (2:6–11), which may be an early Christian hymn that he is quoting. Again this comes out of a real-life situation. He is talking about the unity of the church in Philippi. If we're going to be united, we need humility. Paul quotes Jesus as an example of humility. Jesus, as Paul understands it, was someone with God and in the 'form' of God, that is, part of the reality of God, before he became a human being. Paul then takes a text from the Old Testament prophet Isaiah, where it says that the whole world will bow the knee to the one and only God, the God of Israel (Is. 45:23). Amazingly, Paul applies this to Jesus. Paul would have written this letter within twenty years of Jesus' crucifixion and, if he is quoting a hymn, this might have been written even earlier.

So, within a couple of decades of Jesus' crucifixion, there are Christians of Jewish upbringing and background who are treating Jesus the way that they would treat the God of Israel, whom they worship.

Paul has, of course, been accused of twisting the message of Jesus, the Jew, into a Christ for the Gentiles.

That argument is largely predicated on the grounds that Paul was from Tarsus. He was not a Palestinian Jew but had contact with the Gentile world. Both in the book of Acts and some of Paul's letters there are quotes from Greek poets. But to his pupil Timothy and the Christian church in Corinth, Paul himself talks about the tradition that he has received and passes on (see 1 Cor. 15:3). Some scholars react against this and say that clearly Paul was a creative theologian and did develop Christian theology. But it wasn't a new religion. What he was developing was something that had already started before, and had been handed down to him. He comes into a group of Jews who in their worship are already treating Jesus as if he was divine. And, yes, Paul may well be beginning to conceptualise how it can be that this person who walked around Galilee could, in some sense, be God.

So, in summary, the lowest common denominator among biblical scholars is that Jesus really existed, had the unusual reputation of being a miracle-worker and that within a short period, his followers began to worship him as the Son of God. The next issue is, how do we deal with what is our principal source on Jesus, the New Testament texts and the Gospels in particular, when we're confronted with a host of supernatural stories – which takes us back to Bultmann, who famously said it was impossible to use electric light and the wireless and to believe in spirits and miracles at the same time?[3]

Bultmann said one had to move from the pre-scientific world-view of the Bible to a scientific, Enlightenment world-view and impose it upon the Scriptures. But he equates the mid-twentieth century, scientific world-view with reality, and part of contemporary post-modernism is a reaction against that kind of reality.

But surely most contemporary academics would still share Bultmann's view?

Of course we get those who say that the scientific world-view is *the* world-view and that there is no such thing as supernatural events. Others might say, as scholars we can't talk about supernatural events, because they don't fit into our methodology, but they might still happen.

One of the questions behind all this seems to be whether we can be a Christian even if we don't believe every word in the Bible.

And that's where, in the early twentieth century, we get a fundamentalist reaction against nineteenth-century liberalism. But in a sense, fundamentalism plays liberalism at its own game. Liberals say the Bible can't be accepted because we can't prove it scientifically or historically, and fundamentalists respond by saying that they take it at face value and therefore they must prove its historic and scientific accuracy. They will go to great lengths to try to show that the Bible is true historically and scientifically. But that's the key question: what is truth? Are we to seek to understand the Gospels in terms of twentieth-century history? I think the answer has to be no, because twentieth-century history is linked to one specific, Enlightenment, approach and not to the way people dealt with history in the first century.

How did they write history back then?

Often in a way that lessons could be learnt from it; or as a way of explaining one culture to another culture, as the Jewish, first-century historian, Josephus, did for the Romans. The Gospels clearly have a purpose that is different from writing a modern, quasi-objective biography of Jesus. John, in his Gospel, tells us quite clearly that his purpose of writing is that the reader might know that Jesus is the Christ and believe in him (Jn. 20:31). John has an evangelistic purpose; he is very selective and he tells us that. Luke states that he has talked to eyewitnesses to find certainty for what he has written, so he is claiming that his is a factual account and that he's done his best to ensure that he is reporting accurately what Jesus said and did. But Luke is not writing out of the interest to write accurate history; he wants Theophilus, to whom he is writing, to have his faith affirmed. Matthew's Gospel has five blocks of teachings of Jesus, each with a particular theme to it, but it is very unlikely that these are five original sermons. Much of the teaching in them is found spread around in small chunks in the other Gospels. Matthew was writing as a Jew for a Jewish audience and his five blocks appear to echo the Torah, the five books of Moses, indicating that Jesus is, in a sense, a new Moses, a new teacher. But Matthew also sets out to show that Jesus is descended from Abraham and David and is therefore qualified to be the Messiah. So the Gospels are written with a particular evangelistic purpose and not as objective biographies of Jesus.

Does this element of subjectivity and 'agenda' explain the differences among the Gospels?

Yes, I think it does. The Synoptic Gospels – Matthew, Mark and Luke -– share a lot in common. Virtually everything in Mark is found in Matthew and Luke, so most people think that Matthew and Luke used Mark as one of their sources and rearranged the material to some degree to suit their purposes. So they don't contradict one another; they've simply arranged their material differently and thereby, at times, bring out a different emphasis. That's quite valid; any event or saying might have more than one element of truth. A preacher can use the same anecdote in two different sermons. They can make a different point each time and show different aspects, without changing the content of the anecdote. Then also, because the Gospel writers are selective, they don't always seem to dovetail together. Yet it is possible to produce a composite account that makes sense. In his book, *Who Moved the Stone?*[4] Frank Morison, a lawyer, set out to disprove the veracity of the resurrection accounts in the Gospels because of their differences; instead, he ended up convinced that they were true. As a lawyer he was used to witnesses in court telling different stories about the same event and that's how he came to change his mind about the resurrection accounts.

A few years ago N.T. Wright,[5] in his book, The Resurrection of the Son of God,[6] *seemed to imply that the very fact that the resurrection accounts are not wholly congruent, let alone theologically polished, made them more believable; they read as if someone had told what they had seen, breathless and struggling to make sense of it.*

Going back to the reliability of the Gospels at large, you have talked about the similarities and minor differences between the Synoptic Gospels, Matthew, Mark and Luke. But what of John, which is very different indeed?

John is a much more reflective, consciously theological presentation of Jesus. And for that reason many scholars in the first half of the twentieth century were very unwilling to use John as a historical source. But C.H. Dodd[7] has shown in his book *Historical Tradition in the Fourth Gospel*[8] that there is in fact a firm historical basis for what John is talking about. But John is a theological meditation and the stylistic differences are hard to deny. What we get in John is not so much the direct words of Jesus as in the Synoptic Gospels, where we can translate quite a lot of the Greek back into Aramaic and it seems to be word for word what Jesus would have said; John gives us paraphrases of what Jesus said, seeking to bring out the theology behind them, and embedded in that are the words of Jesus. As a Christian I would want to say, John was inspired by the Spirit to do that. So I see John as a true record of Jesus' teaching if not always of Jesus' own words.

Jesus versus Christ?

Early Christianity is sometimes accused of squeezing the message of Rabbi Jesus into a Hellenistic, pagan mould. A fair criticism?

One of the remarkable discoveries of the second half of the twentieth century was the Jewish character of the Jesus of the Gospels, partly because Jewish scholars were coming in and making that point. Jesus is portrayed as an apocalyptic teacher – one of the strands of first-century Judaism – who is deeply rooted in the Old Testament.

A great deal of what Jesus says of himself can only be fully understood if we have the Old Testament background. The whole idea of Messiah goes back to the Old Testament, although Jesus modifies it by using other Old Testament pictures, especially that of the Suffering Servant, which seems to be echoing Isaiah. Another motif is the one that the Servant would be a light to the Gentiles, according to Isaiah (Is. 42:6). As far as we know, no Jewish teacher before Jesus had linked the Suffering Servant with the Messiah; Jesus brings the two together. In the Last Supper, he seems to equate himself with the Passover lamb and links it to the Exodus event, bringing people not out of political slavery like Moses, but out of spiritual slavery.

Nonetheless, after Jesus' earthly ministry, Paul, the missionary to the Gentiles, had to 'translate' Jesus for non-Jews, and later on the Early Church fathers defined Christianity further in a Greco-Roman context. No doubt that would have affected Christian doctrine?

If Christians want to make the gospel, the good news of Jesus, understandable in their own culture and generation, there's always going to be some translating of the original imagery and concepts. There's always a knife-edge to be walked; how far, in trying to interpret, do you distort?

In his letters, we find the apostle Paul sticking pretty closely with Old Testament concepts and ideas. But he also uses terminology that builds bridges with the Gentile world, for instance his vision of the cosmic Christ in Colossians chapter 1, as the One who is head over the whole universe – terminology that would resonate with the non-Jewish thinker. We also find that at the beginning of John's Gospel, with Jesus as the Word, which reflects the language of the Stoic philosophers as well as Jewish thought.

In the time of the Early Church fathers, the dominant philosophy was some early form of neo-Platonism, so they used Platonic categories. Overall they did a pretty good job, but they also left us some difficult legacies. In the last couple of decades, for example, Christian scholars have been debating what, in technical terms, is called the 'impassibility' of God, which means that God cannot suffer. This goes back to the Platonist idea that if God is perfect he cannot change, because what can something that is perfect change into, other than something that is less than perfect? It's a very static understanding of perfection. Therefore God cannot be changed by anything outside of himself. But that is not the picture of God either in the Old or the New Testament, particularly if we think of Jesus in terms of God suffering on the cross. The early Christians were aware of this problem and tried to meet it in various ways; but I would say they weren't all that successful. Recently, Process Theology and Open Theism have tried to find ways in which God can be both perfect and a being that can respond.

What about the main bone of contention – the divinity of Jesus? Some see in him a gifted Jewish teacher who taught high moral ethics and was made into 'a god' by the church. Others would maintain that the claim to divinity is inherent in his teaching and actions.

When we read the Gospels, it is difficult to deny that Jesus saw himself as more than a human being. He made some amazing statements. People saw an authority in him that was unusual. He said to a paralysed man, 'Son, your sins are forgiven!' The scribes – the experts in Jewish law – and the Pharisees saw this as blasphemy. 'Who can forgive sins but God?' I think they got the point. In the Jewish context, sin was an offence against God. If someone mugged me, I would be very fed up if you forgave them for assaulting me. But Jesus seemed to do that very thing. He didn't even speak like a Hebrew prophet, 'In the name of the Lord I forgive you', or something like that. He just said, 'Your sins are forgiven.' And he made other, similar claims that made him very suspicious in the eyes of the leaders of his day, because it was as if he was acting like God. In Mark 13, he says that heaven and Earth will pass away but his words won't. Now he said that earlier, in the Sermon on the Mount, about the law – the words of God – not passing away. And now he says the same of his own words. He may not actually stand up and say 'I am God!' but he behaves and speaks in ways that imply that he is acting like God. That is the historical basis for the fact that, within ten or twenty years, his followers are worshipping him as God, because they have seen his claim vindicated by his resurrection.

This is what turns Paul around after his experience of the risen Jesus on the Damascus road; that the person who he thought must have been a blasphemer and rightly died on the cross for his blasphemy now sits at the right hand of God. I think that's why, in his letter to the Romans, he talks about Jesus as the one 'declared with power to be the Son of God, by his resurrection from the dead' (Rom. 1:4, NIV). It's the resurrection of Jesus that vindicates his claims. So Paul is not distorting, but developing the gospel message.

In today's society, tolerance is a supreme virtue. As people look back at the Early Church, they point out the debates that went on and certain people being labelled as heretics by those who became the orthodox. There were battles of ideas within the church, both with people who were part of the church, such as Arius (who denied the full deity of Jesus), or people on the fringe of the church, such as the Gnostics. And in the end, the orthodox won. So in that sense, we read theology through the eyes of the orthodox; but that doesn't necessarily mean that the orthodox were wrong. We can assess how true that which became Christian orthodoxy is to the Scriptures and to Jesus. And it is right to ask that question. The systematic theologians, who formulated Christian doctrine, have caused us some problems, but it seems to me that they are truer to the Scriptures than Arius and certainly a lot truer than the Gnostics were. If anyone, it was the Gnostics who clothed what they took from the Christian Scriptures in a Hellenistic philosophy and thereby made Jesus into a second-century, Hellenistic teacher.

Live Full . . .

What kind of world did Jesus grow up in?

When Jesus was born, many Jews were united in the kingdom of Herod the Great, who was, at best, half-Jewish and hated by his Jewish subjects. He became increasingly irrational in his later years. Though we have no evidence of it outside the New Testament, the story about the killing of the baby boys in Bethlehem quite fits Herod's character in his later life, when he became increasingly paranoid and even had some of his family members killed because he thought they were plotting against him.

Jesus came from Galilee. By the time he was growing up, Herod's kingdom had been divided into four parts, including Judea and Galilee. Hellenistic influence in Galilee was strong. The fact that some of Jesus' disciples had Greek names, like Philip and Andrew, shows the influence of Gentile culture. Judea, on the other hand, was much more Hebraic.

Josephus, the first-century Jewish historian, mentions four religious groups. Two of them we know from the New Testament: the Pharisees and the Sadducees. For the Sadducees, the Bible was the Torah, the five books of Moses. The Pharisees accepted as Scripture what we would call the Hebrew Bible, so they believed in things like the resurrection of the dead, which is not mentioned in the Torah but in the books of Daniel and Isaiah.

And unlike the Sadducees, who were more part of the establishment, the Pharisees tried to live counter-culturally in an eager expectance of the kingdom of God.

That's right. The Sadducees were the ruling party that compromised with the Romans, but the Pharisees were the party of the people. They would go into the countryside and preach in the synagogues. Josephus tells us that although the Pharisees were not numerically huge, they had a tremendous influence because of their willingness to go out to the people, who respected their attempt to live holy lives.

Then there were the Zealots, whose hopes centred on the Messiah and the deliverance from the Romans. According to

Josephus, they were found particularly in Galilee, and Josephus himself had been amongst them in his younger days.

The fourth group he mentions are the Essenes, a much more separatist group of which we didn't know much until the 1940s, when the Dead Sea scrolls were found. They seem to have come from a group of Essenes who, most scholars believe, had settled in the ruins of Qumran. They withdrew from mainstream Judaism, because they thought that the temple and the priests were compromised and therefore they regarded the temple as unclean and wouldn't worship there. Instead, they developed their own, parallel Judaism. Some of them seem to have lived in celibate communities, while others were married, and there is now evidence for an Essene community that existed in a particular part of Jerusalem in Jesus' day.

Were the Essenes also a messianic sect?

Yes, but in contrast to the Zealots, they were not politically activist but politically pacifist. They sought to live as a godly community until God would act in his own way and lead them to victory over both the Gentiles and the apostate Jews. Unlike the Zealots, they were not going to initiate this divine intervention.

So, apart from the Sadducees perhaps, everyone loathed the Roman occupation, not only for political but also religious reasons.

It's always hard to generalise at 2,000 years' distance, but this certainly was a difficult province for the Romans to rule, and for many Jews the pagan presence would have been a disgrace. The Judaism of the day was deeply marked by events that had happened over the previous 200 years. Palestine had come under the rule of Alexander the Great. After he died and his empire was divided, Palestine found itself as a frontier province between Egyptian and Mesopotamian and, later, Syrian rule. The Syrian ruler, Antiochus Epiphanies, tried to stamp out Judaism because he found it too troublesome. Judaism at the time was divided over the issue to what extent the Greek culture that Alexander had imported was to be adopted – and because of the in-fighting among the Jews, Antiochus got fed up with them. After all, they were on the border of Egypt and no empire likes its border provinces being unruly. So Antiochus started a severe persecution of the Jews in 165 BC. He desecrated the temple in Jerusalem and dedicated it to Zeus, sacrificing pigs' flesh, which is, of course, anathema to any orthodox Jew. He burnt all the copies of Jewish Scriptures that he could find and banned Sabbath worship and circumcision.

It is out of that kind of experience that the various groups emerged in Jesus' day and, each in their own way, sought to be true to the Judaism of their fathers. The Pharisees stressed the importance of personal holiness. The Essenes rejected the priests in the temple because they were no longer descendants from the tribe of Levi. The Sadducees didn't want to go back to the days of persecution and therefore tried to accommodate the Roman occupants. The Zealots, however, wanted to emulate Judas Maccabaeus, who had managed to end the Syrian persecution and kick out the foreign rulers. So we can see how deeply the Judaism of Jesus' day was influenced, theologically and politically, by the events of 165 BC.

At that point enters a man who proclaims the kingdom of God, and undoubtedly people would have put their hope in him as their political deliverer.

This is why Jesus was always very wary of openly accepting the title 'Messiah' – Christ – and preferred to talk about himself as the Son of Man.

A reference to the Old Testament book of Daniel chapter 7!

The prophet Daniel has a vision of four world empires that are compared to beasts of different sorts. God judges these empires. And 'one like a Son of Man' (Dan. 7:13, NIV) comes to him who receives the kingdom, the power and the glory, and his kingdom is going to last for ever. So the apocalyptic kingdom of God is represented by a human being, which reminds us of Genesis 1 and humans being made in the image of God. The 'one like a Son of Man' is the one that brings to fruition God's purposes in creation and for all humanity. It is significant that Jesus picks up that phrase; it can be understood against the background of Daniel 7 as an apocalyptic way of saying that God's purposes for the world are coming to fruition. But they are God's purposes for the world, not just Judaism, which resonates with the call of Abraham, 'all peoples on earth will be blessed through you' (Gen. 12:3, NIV) and the Servant in Isaiah who becomes a covenant for the Gentiles. So Jesus' use of the Son of Man imagery is not a nationalistic understanding of the kingdom of God but one that embraces all of creation. And indeed, Jesus calls both Matthew the tax collector, who has collaborated with the Romans, and Simon the Zealot to be his disciples.

What part, then, do Jesus' miracles play in his universal, messianic ministry?

The term 'miracle' that we use comes from Latin, meaning something marvellous. The term used in the New Testament is a double term meaning, 'signs and wonders'. Indeed, the things Jesus does are amazing, but perhaps more importantly, they are signs. They point to something. They have a theological message. With our post-Enlightenment background we come to the miracles asking whether they broke the laws of nature. But the issue is: what is their theological message? Some of Jesus' miracles did break the laws of nature. Others, like some of his healings, may indeed have been explicable in natural terms. We are beginning to appreciate how many of our physical ailments are related to our spiritual and emotional state. And if someone is able, by their personality, their presence, to calm someone's physical and emotional state, physical release may follow. So, to me, how exactly we understand some of Jesus' healings isn't all that important; the important thing is what they say about God in Jesus; that, here is somebody who is concerned about people's physical, spiritual and emotional well-being. Here is someone who is ready to battle with spiritual evil. Again, we may want to debate how exactly we understand Jesus' exorcisms and where the boundaries between spiritual and psychological reality are, but the message of the exorcisms is that Jesus came to combat spiritual evil in whatever form it took. But then he was also someone who had influence over the powers of nature – stilling the storm, walking on water – which is what we would expect of the Creator.

So, unless we understand that the spiritual message is the primary message of the miracles, we get caught up with all sorts of questions, such as why Jesus didn't heal everyone. Well, he wasn't there to be a universal doctor; he came to proclaim the kingdom of God.

What, exactly, does the phrase 'kingdom of God' mean?

It would be better to translate 'the reign of God', or 'the rule of God'. It's not a place. It's letting the power of God work in people's lives.

We've looked at Jesus' identity and his miracles. What about his teachings? What was his core message?

The Gospels, certainly the Synoptics (Matthew, Mark and Luke) sum up his message as the kingdom of God being at hand; that people should repent and believe the good news. In other words, as the reign of God comes into the world, people need to change. The word in the original for 'repent' means to turn around. There's something wrong with the world. God's reign is not evident; people aren't accepting him as their sovereign, because there are still powers of evil at work. Jesus proclaims what is technically called an apocalyptic view of the world. Not all rabbis were apocalyptic. Those who were would talk about the prince of darkness, Satan, ruling the world, which made it a rebellious province of God's kingdom, but that the King was coming to reclaim his own territory. They saw the coming of God in terms of the coming of a new age. They talked about the reign of light and the reign of darkness, which is imagery we find in the Gospels. So Jesus comes into the world to reclaim it for God, calling people to turn around and accept the good news he is bringing, namely that there is a God who is sovereign and can release them from the rebellious powers of evil.

Where, then, is the connection between the good news of the kingdom and the Suffering Servant?

The Gospels contain so-called Passion predictions. Scholars may debate how far their actual wording comes from Jesus but they all seem to be in agreement on Jesus' understanding that, for him, bringing in the kingdom of God would mean suffering. Again, here's an analogy with the Old Testament prophets; the Suffering Servant in Isaiah (Is. 53) is very much a prophetic figure, echoing the prophets who suffered for proclaiming the reign of God.

You said that one of the hallmarks of the teachings of the apocalyptic rabbis was their dualist world-view of light and darkness. Could this have been a legacy from Babylonian religion, going back to the days when the Jews were conquered by the Babylonians and led into exile?

You are referring to the influence of Zoroastrianism.

Indeed!

Zoroaster was a prophet among the Indo-European peoples and his thoughts spread into Persia and India. He did teach the dualism of a god of light and a god of darkness being at battle with one another. As for the time when Zoroastrianism became the dominant religion in Persia, most scholars would feel that it was not at the time of the Babylonian exile of the Jews but later, when Persia became the dominant empire, that Zoroastrianism entered Western Persia and became the state religion. So, if it had an influence on the Jews, it would have been in the inter-Testamental period, which, to be fair, is when we see more apocalyptic imagery being used.

  Some of the increased dualistic imagery of light and darkness was probably influenced by the Jews of the Diaspora who had been in contact with Zoroastrianism. However, this was not a radical departure from the Old Testament, but a developing of something that was already there, if in a less clear form. The imagery of light and dark for good and bad is a natural imagery that people have used in many cultures.

Overall, in the Old Testament, there seems to be a striking absence of heaven and hell, which is a key feature of Zoroastrianism and very prominent in the teachings of Jesus and in the New Testament as such.

In the Old Testament, the idea appears in Daniel 12:2. On the whole, the Old Testament speaks of Sheol, the place of the dead. There seems to be a developing understanding of Sheol in the Old Testament; in some places it appears to be little more than an undifferentiated place of the dead, where there is no real sense of an ongoing life. The psalmist says that those in Sheol cannot praise God (Ps. 6:5; 30:9) and Ecclesiastes states that in Sheol there is no knowledge (Eccl. 9:10). But then we also find the psalmist saying that his relationship with God is so real that even death can't bring it to an end. 'At Your right hand are pleasures forevermore' (Ps. 16:11, NKJV).

In Isaiah and Ezekiel, we come across resurrection imagery, though more as a symbol of revival of the nation than individual resurrection. In Isaiah 53, there is the implication that the Suffering Servant knows after his death that he has been vindicated; how would he know if he's still dead? Job says that he knows that his Redeemer lives and seems to expect to be aware of his vindication beyond death (Job 19:25–27). And finally, in Daniel 12, we have a clear statement about resurrection to eternal life and resurrection to some kind of punishment (v.2).

But would prophets of the exile, such as Daniel, not have been in touch with Zoroastrianism and its dualistic world-view?

Probably not; certainly not Isaiah or Ezekiel; with Daniel it depends on when we date the book. One of the central ideas of the Old Testament is the justice of God. Job battles with the idea that the wicked don't always get their comeuppance in this life, but he does come to the assurance that God will somehow sort it out. As for Daniel, he deals with the question of what happens to the martyrs, those who have died for their faith, and the ideas of justice beyond death and heaven and hell imply that they didn't die in vain. At the end of the day, who knows, maybe God did use the interaction of the Jews with Zoroastrianism, so they would recognise that there is a justice beyond death.

. . . Die Young

The earthly ministry of Jesus ends on the cross. On the surface, we can see his death as a result of the religious leaders wanting to avoid religious trouble, and the political leaders wanting to avoid political trouble. But Jesus himself and, at a later stage, his followers came to see the cross as something of much deeper significance.

The New Testament writers refer to Old Testament imagery to understand that deeper meaning. Jesus uses the language of ransom and redemption, the idea that people are set free from slavery by someone paying a price for their freedom. He says that the Son of Man will 'give his life as a ransom for many' (Mk. 10:45, NIV), and the apostles Paul and Peter pick up the language of redemption, of freeing from slavery, in their writings. So Jesus' death is seen as the price for freedom, not from the powers of Rome, but from the powers of evil. At the Last Supper that imagery is linked with Passover. This goes back to the story of Exodus, in which God judges the Egyptians, who have held the Jews in slavery, by killing their firstborns. The Hebrew slaves sacrifice a lamb in the place of the firstborn son. At the Last Supper, Jesus seems to be identifying himself with the sacrificial lamb: 'This is my body; this is my blood.' Paul talks about Christ, our Passover sacrifice (1 Cor. 5:7). Jews were used to sacrificing animals for the forgiveness of sins.

Paul uses the language of justification, which is an imagery taken from law courts and goes back to the Old Testament idea of God being our judge. God is able to declare people acquitted in court, and this is made possible by Jesus' death. Paul also talks about reconciliation, which is more of a personal relationship type language.

People nowadays seem to struggle, possibly more than they used to, with the concept of Jesus dying for the sins of humanity – essentially in three ways. The idea of a blood sacrifice seems repulsive; the idea that God should vent his wrath on an innocent victim appears unjust and unethical. And the idea of redemptive violence has served as a justification for religiously motivated violence.

And I suppose, fourthly, people find the idea of God's wrath as such very difficult. We can only think about God in picture language, drawn from human experience, which is the most complex one we know and therefore comes closest to God. We're happy to talk about God's love but we feel less comfortable with God's anger, because in our human experience anger is often vindictive and destructive, and therefore we don't like to use it of God. Yet there is, to use biblical terminology, 'righteous anger'. If I didn't feel angry when I read about people in other parts of the world being oppressed, children being used as slave workers, or about the trafficking of women as sex slaves from Eastern into Western Europe – if none of that made me angry, you would say there was something morally wrong with me. It is in that sense that the Bible talks about the wrath of God. God is concerned about right and wrong. God's wrath is a flip side of his love, his deep concern for his creation.

As for blood sacrifice, for an ancient Israelite having to sacrifice a perfectly healthy sheep or goat or other animal was a costly thing to do. The average person would not have herded many sheep or goats. To sacrifice one of them was to pay a huge price. It brought home to the people the importance of commitment to the moral standards of the God they worshipped. Sacrifices in the Old Testament are not used to manipulate God, but as gifts of praise or as recognition of imperfection and sinfulness, which needs to be dealt with.

When we come to the cross, the striking thing is that the Gospel accounts say very little about the physical suffering. They don't make a great thing about it as a blood sacrifice and, in my view, it is something of a distortion to make so much of the physical torture. Of course, crucifixion was a horrible thing, but that is not played upon in the New Testament. What is stressed is the obedience of Jesus, the Suffering Servant. Jesus struggles with the cross in the Garden of Gethsemane but, as Paul says in Philippians 2, he humbles himself and is obedient even unto death (v.8). The emphasis is on his willingness to suffer; suffering without obedience would have meant nothing. This is where the understanding of the cross in terms of redemptive violence is a misunderstanding if not indeed a misrepresentation. It's not that God saves the world by violence; it's that Jesus saves the world by obedience. The Suffering Servant of Isaiah is the key thing; a servant is obedient to his calling.

What of the fact that God punishes an innocent victim; does that not make God morally inferior to human beings?

It is not God arbitrarily taking an innocent victim and punishing him. It is God himself who takes the consequences of his own law on the cross. God himself, in Christ, reconciles the world to himself. In Christ, God shows how seriously he takes his own standards, firstly by living according to them and secondly, by taking the consequences of humans not meeting them upon himself. Forgiveness of the human trespassing of God's moral laws is not saying, 'It doesn't matter what you have done.' The offer of forgiveness is made through the cross. The message is, 'If you are prepared to confess that you have not lived by God's laws and that you deserve the consequences that Christ took upon himself, and if you are prepared to change your way of life, you have free forgiveness. And beyond that, you have the power of the Holy Spirit to enable you to live God's way.'

Is personal redemption the only way of interpreting the cross?

The New Testament writers use several pictures. The cross can be seen, as someone has said, like a diamond with many facets, as long as we see them as complementary pictures and keep to the heart of the matter; that there is an act of God to deal with the wrongs in human life and society and to triumph over them. As a pastor, I have found that the picture of justification speaks to people who have a sense of guilt and feel that they are not good enough. On the other hand, the Christus victor image – that Jesus, through his unconquerable love for humanity, triumphs over the powers of evil that try to wipe him out – may speak to people who feel entrapped by something more powerful than them, be it an addiction or whatever, and who need to know that there is a power that can deliver them. And to those who feel alienated from the world, Paul's language of the reconciliation of the cosmos makes sense, and so on. It's important to keep all of these pictures alive.

The Faith   101

Risen Indeed?

*The passage 1 Corinthians 15:3–8 is generally recognised to be the ear-
liest source that talks about Jesus coming back from the dead. But in the
passage, Paul neither mentions the empty tomb nor the women who,
according to the Gospels, were the first to find the tomb empty. Did Paul
and the Gospel writers draw from different resurrection traditions?*

Paul lived in a very patriarchal culture. Normally, in the law courts
a woman's testimony was not acceptable. So who is going to
weaken their case by using unacceptable witnesses? By contrast, in
the Gospels, women are the first to see the empty tomb and to meet
the risen Jesus, which says something about the importance that
God put on them, while the culture of the time didn't. Paul is writing some twenty years after the event, and he says he is quoting
the tradition he passes on to the believers (1 Cor. 15:3); in other
words, the tradition goes back earlier than Paul.

I think the reason that the empty tomb is not mentioned by Paul
is that it is implied. In Jewish thinking, resurrection meant nothing if it wasn't resurrection of the body. There is not the strongly
dualist division between body and spirit of the Greeks, for whom
existence beyond death was purely spiritual; in the Jewish tradition, the idea was bodily resurrection. In the Old Testament a
human being is not seen in a dualistic, but a holistic way. So when
Paul talks about the risen Christ, he too means bodily resurrection. Notice that he quotes the tradition that Jesus was raised on
the third day (1 Cor. 15:4) – but how would anyone have known
if the tomb had not been found to be empty on that day?

*Now, let's look at the resurrection accounts in the Gospels. There are
obvious differences. For instance, Mark, at least in what appears to be
the original version, breaks off where the women find the empty tomb,
without any mention of them meeting the risen Jesus. Luke's geography
seems somewhat peculiar, as he focuses on Jerusalem after the resurrection, not Galilee like the other Evangelists. What are we to make of these
incongruities?*

The ending of Mark's Gospel has been a puzzle down through
the years. Did Mark intend to stop where the Gospel we have

today ends? Did he intend to end with the women's amazement and fear? After all, Mark is a bit like a detective story, and leaving us at the end with this sense of something amazing happening of course makes sense in the light of Jesus' earlier prediction of his suffering, death and resurrection. So Mark may have left this 'open ending' for the reader to draw their own conclusions. Other people think that we have lost the original ending of Mark's Gospel, whereas scholars have concluded that the ending we now have in our Bibles is a compendium of the appearances of the risen Jesus as they are described in the other Gospels.

In what way does the 'new ending' differ from the rest of Mark's Gospel?

There are differences in style and vocabulary, and it does seem to be a compendium of what we have in the other Gospels.

There are, then, some differences when we compare Matthew, Luke and John, but it is possible to put the pieces of the jigsaw together; we have complementary, rather than contradictory accounts, according to the different experiences of individuals which were passed down to the Gospel writers through different traditions.

In the past, people who looked at the resurrection accounts through a naturalist, Enlightenment lens, tried to come up with various, alternative explanations. Are those still taken seriously among scholars today? Some have argued, for example, that Jesus fainted on the cross and recovered in the coldness of the tomb.

The problem with that is three or four women could not have moved the stone in front of the tomb, which, we are told, was guarded. And yet, the theory implies that a badly wounded and weakened man could have done that very thing and would thereafter convince his followers that he was the victorious one who had returned from the dead.

Could the disciples have gone to the wrong grave?

We are told that some of the women had stayed at the cross, very likely until Jesus was taken down, and that they had gone to the tomb where Jesus' body had been put by Joseph of Arimathea. The women then went back to the tomb within forty-eight hours; it's unlikely that they would have picked the wrong one. The Jewish leaders and the Roman authorities knew which tomb was the right one and they could have quickly scotched the rumour of the resurrection if the body had still been in the tomb.

What about the claim that Jesus' disciples had stolen the body?

The nearest disciples of Jesus were prepared to suffer and die for the message that Jesus was the risen King of kings; why suffer and die for something you know to be a hoax you yourself have created?

Could the intense grief over Jesus' death have triggered a collective vision of their beloved master returning from the dead?

Initially, the disciples didn't believe in the resurrection. That's not what we expect of wish-fulfilment; they would have embraced the women's message with open arms. Instead, they were afraid and unbelieving, the supreme example being Thomas. They did not expect resurrection.

Also, the resurrection accounts are too varied to fit into a psychological pattern. Sometimes Jesus appears to one person (Jn. 20:10ff.), sometimes to a small group of people (Lk. 24:13ff.), once in a locked room (Jn. 20:19), then by the seashore (Jn. 21). Paul mentions an occasion where over five hundred people were gathered when Jesus appeared to them (1 Cor. 15:6). There is no single, 'collective vision' that could be explained away in psychological terms.

What, then, if anything, makes the resurrection believable, not as a mythical or symbolic, but as a real, historic, event?

At the core of the accounts are the empty tomb and the meetings with the risen Christ. There was a man, Jesus, who died on a cross, and forty-eight hours – or three days in Jewish counting – later we have an empty tomb, and this Jesus is appearing to people who see that he is recognisably the same person and yet different.

In a sense, the resurrection is a bit like a scientific hypothesis, in that we have various objections to disprove it, which, as we have seen, fail to make sense of the event. The thing that does make sense of the empty tomb and the meetings with the risen Jesus is his own claim that he was not just a man, but God incarnate and able to defeat death.

In our culture, we tend to think, if at all, of the afterlife in terms of our souls continuing to exist in some nebulous state, while our bodies decay. This makes the gospel claim of the bodily resurrection of Jesus all the harder to grasp.

Paul grapples with this in 1 Corinthians 15. In Corinth, some believers found the concept of the resurrection too much to take, probably because they had a Platonic background, based on the idea that matter is in some sense evil and corrupt and that therefore, when one goes to the realm of the perfect when one dies, it can't be one's body; it's just the spirit. Paul rejects that. Resurrection, as he understands it, is a mixture of continuity and discontinuity. He uses the picture of a seed that produces a plant; there is a connection between the two, but they are not the same. The risen body is a transformed body. Jesus was recognisable, bearing the marks of crucifixion; yet this was clearly not the same as the physical body that had been laid in the tomb.

The resurrection of Jesus foreshadows the resurrection of believers to eternal life with God. Does this imply that if Jesus had remained in the grave, the Christian faith would be worthless?

That's what Paul says (1 Cor. 15:14). Going back to Jesus' Son of Man imagery, his work is not just saving individual souls, but completing God's work in creation. That is where the significance of the transformed resurrection body lies, because the material creation is neither devalued nor discarded by God. His saving purpose involves the bringing of creation to its completion. That's where the biblical language of restored creation, of a new heaven and a new Earth, is so important.

But doesn't the New Testament also talk about this present world being destroyed in the end?

I think that is a misunderstanding of 2 Peter 3:10. The language and imagery goes back to the Old Testament. The motif of purifying fire is found in Isaiah, for instance (Is. 48:10), and in Malachi (Mal. 3:2). So Peter seems to be talking not about a fire that will destroy the cosmos but one that will purify it. And, when the book of Revelation talks about a new heaven and a new Earth, the reader needs to know that there are two words in the Greek for 'new' – one means something that didn't exist before, the other means something that is new in quality. And that is the word that is used consistently in the New Testament with regard to the new heaven and the new Earth. It's about a new quality, not something that didn't exist before.

I like the term Sir John Polkinghorne[9] uses. He talks about creatio ex vetere, not ex nihilo; God's new creation is out of the old, not out of nothing.

This has ethical implications!

Indeed. The new heaven and the new Earth, in Revelation, are seen in terms of a new city, the New Jerusalem. In Genesis 1 we begin with a garden made by God. The first city is made by Cain (Gen. 4:17), who murdered his brother. So the city is always a bit ambiguous in the Bible. And yet, in the end, what we have is a garden city. The Tree of Life is in the New Jerusalem, as it was in the Garden of Eden; so is the river of life. But the New Jerusalem is also something that humans have contributed to. So all we do in this life and this world, God takes up, purifies by burning the dross, and uses what is good in the new, transformed creation. What we do in this life has eternal importance.

So is the New Testament meaning of heaven not some place in space but rather Earth renewed?

As we have seen before, when Jesus ascends to heaven, rather than taking off into space like a rocket, he disappears into a cloud. In the Bible, the cloud is a symbol of God appearing. The ascension, therefore, is more like Jesus fading out of the picture, rather than going to another, physical place in this cosmos. And I think it's helpful to think of the new heaven and the new Earth in terms of a transformed cosmos. The language of Revelation seems to say not that we go to a heavenly place, but that God will come to a renewed Earth.

A Final Thought

I pointed out at the beginning that my conversation on faith and science with Reverend Dr Ernest Lucas would dissatisfy readers who were either challenging us to offer a seamless, rational argument for the existence of God or, on the other hand, to debunk modern cosmology and biology as blasphemous world-views and to refute them by presenting the foundations for traditional Christian belief as a bullet-proof fact file, and a literalist interpretation of the Bible as the only valid one. If one of these was what you expected, we have failed. But I do hope that the preceding pages have shown a number of things –

1. that it is not irrational to believe in an ultimate mover behind the universe and life on Earth; that, while classic design arguments may no longer hold, the question why there is not nothing is still a pressing one;
2. that the fine-tuning of the universe and the components of life on Earth, though dismissed by some as chance events, can just as well be attributed to a supreme cosmic intelligence;
3. that the God of the Bible is bigger than, and different from, the designer god that sceptics disparage by pointing to the progress of science and the closing gaps in our understanding of nature;
4. that our spiritual significance is not necessarily undermined by the fact that we have been shoved from the physical 'centre' of the universe (which, in fact, does not exist as such);
5. that evolutionary biology is neither the bedrock for an irrefutable atheist position, nor a demonic ploy to deceive the faithful;

6. that a figurative reading of the creation account in Genesis can be defended by biblical scholarship without denying the message of there being a creator who made man and woman in his image;

7. that Jesus was not only a historic figure, but that the Gospel witness of him being the Son of God is coherent in itself, and that his resurrection from the dead – the event that would vindicate the outrageous claim – is not purely a matter of personal belief but can, to some degree, be approached through rational enquiry.

Points one to six may be interesting, even intriguing, but no more. Point seven is the crucial one. We remain lost in speculation unless God shows himself. According to the New Testament, he has. The gospel message of God's self-revelation in Christ goes not only way beyond the moral designer god of natural theology, but also any other, humanly motivated, religious quest. The issue, then, is whether that message is an utter delusion, a pernicious deception, or indeed the key to approaching and knowing God. C.S. Lewis' plain argument springs to mind that, in claiming divinity, Jesus was either mad, bad or God.[1] The fourth option – that he was honestly convinced of his divine nature but mistaken – is so close to the first one that it does not really qualify as an option at all; sincere, but misguided, belief in one's own divinity would not appear on any sane person's radar screen.

The task, then, is to soberly examine the claim of Christ in the light of his teachings and actions. Again, we are invited to approach faith with an open mind, while realising that when all is said, any human attempt to comprehend God, even God incarnate, will be limited. As the apostle Paul, who was anything but coy about his convictions, put it, we only know in part (1 Cor. 13:9). We can 'think God', but only so far. There is room for the critical probing of the mind as well as mystery, humility, and faith.

Endnotes

The Issue

[1] P. Harrison, *The Bible, Protestantism, and the Rise of Natural Science* (Cambridge: Cambridge University Press, 1998).

[2] Italian mathematician and philosopher (1564–1642).

[3] German astronomer (1571–1630); his planetary laws prepared the way for Newton.

[4] Polish astronomer (1473–1543) who toppled Ptolemy's heliocentric system.

[5] Galileo disproved Aristotle's theories about falling objects and why some things float and others don't. More critically, Galileo questioned his assumption that the Earth does not move.

[6] Francis Bacon (1561–1626), founder of Empiricism, in *Novum organum scientiorum* (1620).

[7] No doubt one of the most influential Christian theologians and philosophers (1225–74).

[8] A fourth-century bishop (Hippo Regius, North Africa), church father and arguably the most influential Western theologian.

[9] German playwright (1898–1956).

[10] The father of classical physics (1643–1727), who reigned supreme until the advent of the theory of relativity and quantum physics.

[11] French mathematician and astronomer (1749–1827), in *Exposition du système du monde* (1796).

[12] Evolutionary biologist and popular, atheist author (born 1941).

[13] Pierre Abélard (1079–1141) applied the principles of logical enquiry to Christian theology.

[14] William of Ockham's (circa 1285–circa 1349/50) philosophy was grounded in Christianity and the Bible, but his philosophical

approach of keeping knowledge separate from belief eventually contributed to driving a wedge between faith and science. The principle known as Ockam's Razor states that simple philosophical explanations are better than complex hypotheses.

[15] René Descartes (1596–1650) based philosophy on epistemology (theory of knowledge), rather than metaphysics.

[16] Bishop of Alexandria (fourth century).

[17] In T. Adams, 'Masters of the Universe', *The Observer* (17.9.06), Review, p.4.

[18] Swiss theologian (1886–1968), who stressed the supremacy of God's self-revelation over and above any human, religious quest.

[19] Scottish philosopher and historian (1711–76).

[20] Francis Bacon had argued for studying small areas of reality and inducing an overall pattern on the basis of what you observed.

[21] Karl Popper (1902–94), Austrian-British philosopher, *The Logic of Scientific Discovery* (New York: Basic Books, 1959).

[22] R. Dawkins, 'A Survival Machine', in J. Brookman (ed.), *The Third Culture*. Quoted in A. McGrath, *Dawkins' God: Genes, Memes and the Meaning of Life* (Oxford: Blackwell, 2005), p.146.

[23] Hungarian-British scientist and philosopher (1891–1976).

1. – The Sky

[1] British astronomer (1915–2001).

[2] There are four of these: gravity, electromagnetism and two forces which operate at the atomic level, called the strong and weak force.

[3] Paul Davis, *The Mind of God* (London: Simon & Schuster Limited, 1992), p.191.

[4] Stephen Hawking, *A Brief History of Time* (London: Bantam, 1988).

[5] German philosopher and polymath (1646–1716).

[6] Soviet cosmonaut (1934–68); the first man in space.

2. – The Cell

[1] From the opening of Darwin's *The Origin of Species* (1859).

[2] French eighteenth-century naturalists who proposed a link between natural environment and biological change.

³ William Paley, Archdeacon of Carlisle, Christian apologist (1743–1805).
⁴ Scottish geologist (1797–1875).
⁵ Thomas Robert Malthus, English national economist (1766–1834).
⁶ General revolutionary movement throughout the Continent of Europe.
⁷ English biologist known as 'Darwin's bulldog' (1825–95).
⁸ Augustinian prior and naturalist (1822–84), whose rules of inheritance remained unnoticed by scientists during his – and Darwin's – lifetime.
⁹ Third century church father whose theology influenced mainly the Eastern Church.
¹⁰ William A. Dembski, US mathematician; one of the chief proponents of Intelligent Design (born 1960).
¹¹ William A. Dembski, *The Design Inference* (Cambridge: Cambridge University Press, 1998).
¹² Born 1952.
¹³ Newton's view that the solar system required divine intervention to remain stable was refuted by Laplace.
¹⁴ French anthropologist and theologian (1881–1955).
¹⁵ Second century, Greek, church father who sought to defend Christianity against the influence of Gnosticism.
¹⁶ French biochemist (1910–76); discovered the control function of regulatory genes over 'normal' genes.
¹⁷ Jacques Monod, *Chance and Necessity: An Essay on the Natural Philosophy of Modern Biology* (New York: Alfred A. Knopf, 1971).
¹⁸ Peter Atkins, professor of chemistry and author who writes and speaks on what he regards as the incompatibility of science and religion (born 1940).

3. – The Faith

¹ German philosopher (1889–1976), influenced French existentialism (Sartre).
² Regarded as the father of 'liberal theology' (1768–1834).
³ Rudolf Bultmann, *Neues Testament und Mythologie* (1941). (English version London: SCM, 1985).
⁴ Frank Morison, *Who Moved the Stone?* (London: Faber & Faber Limited, 1930).

⁵ New Testament scholar; Bishop of Durham (born 1948).
⁶ N.T. Wright, *The Resurrection of the Son of God* (London: SPCK, 2003).
⁷ Welsh New Testament scholar (1884–1973).
⁸ C.H. Dodd, *Historical Tradition in the Fourth Gospel* (Cambridge: Cambridge University Press, 1963).
⁹ English physicist and theologian (born 1930).

A Final Thought

¹ See C.S. Lewis, *Mere Christianity* (First published 1952; First issued in Fontana Books 1955. Reprinted in Fount Paperbacks May 1977. Twenty-fifth impression May 1989, London: Collins 1989).